SIDE by SIDE

Extra

Book & eText ❹

- Expanded Grammar
- Self-Tests & Skill Checks
- Digital FunZone & Audio

Steven J. Molinsky • Bill Bliss

Illustrated by Richard E. Hill

Side by Side Extra Book & eText 4

Pearson Education, 10 Bank Street, White Plains, NY 10606

Staff credits: The people who make up the *Side by Side Extra* team, representing content creation, design, manufacturing, marketing, multimedia, project management, publishing, rights management, and testing are Pietro Alongi, Allen Ascher, Rhea Banker, Elizabeth Barker, Lisa Bayrasli, Elizabeth Carlson, Jennifer Castro, Tracey Munz Cataldo, Diane Cipollone, Aerin Csigay, Victoria Denkus, Dave Dickey, Daniel Dwyer, Wanda España, Oliva Fernandez, Warren Fischbach, Pam Fishman, Nancy Flaggman, Patrice Fraccio, Irene Frankel, Aliza Greenblatt, Lester Holmes, Janet Johnston, Caroline Kasterine, Barry Katzen, Ray Keating, Renee Langan, Jaime Lieber, José Antonio Méndez, Julie Molnar, Alison Pei, Pamela Pia, Stuart Radcliffe, Jennifer Raspiller, Kriston Reinmuth, Mary Perrotta Rich, Tania Saiz-Sousa, Katherine Sullivan, Paula Van Ells, Kenneth Volcjak, and Wendy Wolf.

Contributing authors: Laura English, Meredith Westfall

Text composition: TSI Graphics, Inc.

Illustrations: Richard E. Hill

Photo credits: Page 47 (top right) Everett Collection Historical/Alamy, (top left) Corbis, (middle right) Morphart/Fotolia, (middle left) Pictorial Press Ltd/Alamy, (bottom right) Pictorial Press Ltd/Alamy, (bottom left) akg-images/Newscom; p. 48 (top left) donyanedomam/Fotolia, (top middle) Konstantin Kulikov/Fotolia, (top right) Gail Johnson/Fotolia, (middle left) rnl/Fotolia, (middle) Rudolf Tepfenhart/Fotolia, (middle right) MasterLu/Fotolia, (bottom left) tonyv3112/Fotolia, (bottom middle) Heritage Image Partnership Ltd/Alamy, (bottom right) Russell Kord/Alamy; p. 49 Rafael Ben-Ari/Fotolia; p. 79 (top left) WENN.com/Newscom, (top right) ZUMA Press, Inc./Alamy, (middle left) AP Images, (middle right) Everett Collection, (bottom left) ZUMA Press, Inc./Alamy, (bottom right) Bettmann/Corbis, (far bottom left) Pictorial Press Ltd/Alamy; p. 80 (clover) Jon Beard/Shutterstock, (moon) Lynne Carpenter/Shutterstock, (well) SW Productions/Stockbyte/Getty Images, (candles) Dmitry Vereshchagin/Fotolia, (nut) Mamuka/Fotolia, (grape) DLeonis/Fotolia, (leaf) Springfield Gallery/Fotolia, (lightning) valdezrl/Fotolia, (wishbone) Blend Images/Shutterstock, (full moon) jovica antoski/Fotolia, (fountain) art_zzz/Fotolia, (star) Jill Fromer/Photodisc/Getty Images; p. 81 (top left) Andres Rodriguez/Fotolia, (top middle) George Wada/Fotolia, (top right) Aaron Amat/Fotolia, (left) Kadmy/Fotolia, (bottom left) Vibe Images/Fotolia, (bottom middle) Monkey Business/Fotolia, (bottom right) Christopher Meder/Fotolia; p. 125 Monkey Business/Fotolia; p. 126 (top left) Gino Santa Maria/Fotolia, (top right) nyul/Fotolia, (bottom left) Top Photo Corporation/Top Photo/Corbis, (bottom middle) apops/Fotolia, (bottom right) Tetra images RF/Getty Images; p. 127 Media Bakery13/Shutterstock; p. 159 (top left) Ewing Galloway/Alamy, (top right) Stephen Coburn/Fotolia, (bottom left) ClassicStock/Alamy, (bottom right) AVAVA/Shutterstock; p. 160 (top left) Susan Liebold/Alamy, (top right) YOSHIKAZU TSUNO/AFP/Newscom, (top middle left) HUY NGUYEN/KRT/Newscom, (top middle right) Schalk van Zuydam/AP Images, (bottom middle left) apops/Fotolia, (bottom middle right) Alvey & Towers Picture Library/Alamy, (bottom left) David Eulitt/KRT/Newscom, (bottom right) sima/Fotolia; p. 161 (top left) Hero Images/Getty Images, (top middle) Ulrich Baumgarten/Getty Images, (top right) michaeljung/Fotolia, (left) Jacek Chabraszewski/Fotolia, (bottom left) Darren Baker/Fotolia, (bottom middle) B. Boissonnet/BSIP/Corbis, (bottom right) spotmatik/Shutterstock.

The authors gratefully acknowledge the contribution of Tina Carver in the development of the original *Side by Side* program.

Library of Congress Cataloging-in-Publication Data

Names: Molinsky, Steven J., author. | Bliss, Bill, author.
Title: Side by side extra : book & etext / Steven J. Molinsky ; Bill Bliss.
Description: Third Edition. | White Plains, NY : Pearson Education, [2016] |
  Includes index.
Identifiers: LCCN 2015025510| ISBN 9780132458849 | ISBN 9780132458856 |
  ISBN 9780132458863 | ISBN 9780132458887 | ISBN 9780134306513 |
  ISBN 9780134308265
Subjects: LCSH: English language--Conversation and phrase books. | English
  language--Textbooks for foreign speakers.
Classification: LCC PE1131 .M576 2016 | DDC 428.3/4--dc23
LC record available at http://lccn.loc.gov/2015025510

Side by Side Extra Book & eText 4: ISBN 13 – 978-0-13-245888-7; ISBN 10 – 0-13-245888-8
1 2 3 4 5 6 7 8 9 10–V082–22 21 20 19 18 17 16 15

Side by Side Extra Book & eText with Audio CD 4: ISBN 13 – 978-0-13-430669-8; ISBN 10 – 0-13-430669-4
1 2 3 4 5 6 7 8 9 10–V082–22 21 20 19 18 17 16 15

Side by Side Extra Book & eText International 4: ISBN 13 – 978-0-13-430649-0; ISBN 10 – 0-13-430649-X
1 2 3 4 5 6 7 8 9 10–V082–22 21 20 19 18 17 16 15

Printed in the United States of America

CONTENTS

1

Review:
Present Perfect Tense
Present Perfect Continuous Tense
Past Perfect Tense
Past Perfect Continuous Tense

- Describing Actions That Have Occurred
- Describing Actions That Haven't Occurred Yet
- Discussing Duration of Activity
- Discussing Things People Had Done

VOCABULARY PREVIEW

Things to Do Today

☐ take inventory

☐ write a report

☐ speak to the boss

☐ go to the bank

☐ eat lunch

☐ give out the paychecks

☐ set up the meeting room

☐ see the personnel officer

☐ get gas

☐ drive to the gym

☐ swim

☐ do sit-ups

Things I've Done Today: I've . . .

☑ 1. taken inventory
☑ 2. written a report
☑ 3. spoken to the boss
☑ 4. gone to the bank

☑ 5. eaten lunch
☑ 6. given out the paychecks
☑ 7. set up the meeting room
☑ 8. seen the personnel officer

☑ 9. gotten gas
☑ 10. driven to the gym
☑ 11. swum
☑ 12. done sit-ups

I've Sung for Many Years

(I have)	I've
(We have)	We've
(You have)	You've
(They have)	They've
(He has)	He's
(She has)	She's
(It has)	It's

eaten.

A. Can you sing?

B. Yes. I've sung for many years.

1. *swim*
   swum

2. *draw pictures*
   drawn

3. *drive trucks*
   driven

4. *speak French*
   spoken

5. *fly airplanes*
   flown

6. *take inventory*
   taken

7. *grow corn*
   grown

8. *ride horses*
   ridden

9. *write speeches*
   written

Have You Eaten Lunch Yet?

Have { I / we / you / they } eaten?
Has { he / she / it }

Yes, { I / we / you / they } have.
{ he / she / it } has.

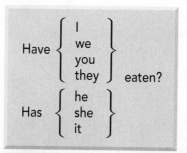

eat
ate
eaten

eat lunch

A. Have you **eaten** lunch yet?

B. Yes, I have. I **ate** lunch a little while ago.

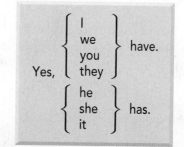

write
wrote
written

write her composition

A. Has Tina **written** her composition yet?

B. Yes, she has. She **wrote** her composition a little while ago.

go
went
gone

1. *you*
   go to the post office

give
gave
given

2. *Dan*
   give out the paychecks

take
took
taken

3. *you and Susan*
   take a break

do
did
done

4. *you*
   do Room 24

see
saw
seen

5. *the employees*
   see the new copy machine

feed
fed
fed

6. *Michael*
   feed the monkeys

No, They Haven't

| Have | I, we, you, they | eaten? |
| Has | he, she, it | |

| No, | I, we, you, they | haven't. |
| | he, she, it | hasn't. |

| I, We, You, They | haven't (have not) | eaten. |
| He, She, It | hasn't (has not) | |

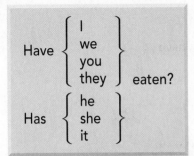

give
gave
given

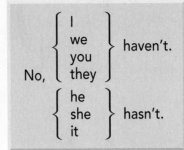

go
went
gone

A. Have you **given** blood recently?

B. No, I haven't. I haven't **given** blood in a long time.

A. Has your father **gone** fishing recently?

B. No, he hasn't. He hasn't **gone** fishing in a long time.

write
wrote
written

1. *you*
   write in your journal

be
was/were
been

2. *Dorothy*
   be sick

get
got
gotten

3. *your son*
   get a haircut

run
ran
run

4. *you and your wife*
   run in a marathon

have
had
had

5. *you*
   have a medical checkup

wear
wore
worn

6. *Anthony*
   wear his tuxedo

4

How Long?

for	since
five years	five o'clock
a week	last week
a long time	2001
many years	he started college

A. How long have you known how to water-ski?

B. I've known how to water-ski for many years.

A. How long has Alexander been a vegetarian?

B. He's been a vegetarian since he started college.

1. *be married*
ten years

2. *have a toothache*
ten o'clock this morning

3. *be in the hospital*
last week

4. *own this car*
thirty-two years

5. *have a British accent*
she moved to London

6. *know each other*
2001

7. *play the violin*
he was in first grade

8. *like hip hop music*
a long time

9. *want to be an actress*
she was four years old

5

READING

A VERY BUSY DAY AT THE OFFICE

Things to Do Today
- ☑ go to the bank
- ☐ take the mail to the post office
- ☐ write my monthly report
- ☑ meet with the personnel officer about my maternity leave
- ☐ speak to the boss about my salary
- ☑ send a fax to the company's office in Tokyo
- ☐ read the office manager's memo about recycling
- ☐ see the training video about the new computer system

Allison is having a very busy day at the office. She has done some of the things she has to do today, but there are many other things she hasn't done yet. She has gone to the bank, but she hasn't taken the mail to the post office yet. She also hasn't written her monthly report. She has already met with the personnel officer about her maternity leave, but she hasn't spoken to the boss yet about her salary. She has sent a fax to the company's office in Tokyo. She hasn't read the office manager's memo about recycling. And she hasn't seen the training video about the new computer system. Allison is probably going to stay late at the office today so she can do all the things she hasn't done yet.

 READING *CHECK-UP*

Q & A

Allison's co-workers are asking her about the things she has done today. Using this model, create dialogs based on the story.

A. Allison, have you _____ yet?
B. { Yes, I have. } { No, I haven't. }

LISTENING

Carl is going to have a party at his apartment this Saturday night. This is the list of things that Carl needs to do to get ready for the party. Check the things on the list that Carl has already done.

- ___ go to the supermarket
- ___ clean the apartment
- ___ get balloons at the party store
- ___ buy some new dance music
- ___ hang up the decorations
- ___ make the food
- ___ tell the neighbors about the party
- ___ give the dog a bath

They've Been Dancing for Ten Hours

(I have)	I've
(We have)	We've
(You have)	You've
(They have)	They've
(He has)	He's
(She has)	She's
(It has)	It's

⎫ been working.

A. How long have your friends been dancing?

B. They've been dancing for ten hours.

1. *wait for the bus*
   since 8 o'clock

2. *study*
   for five hours

3. *work here*
   for thirty-five years

4. *argue*
   since we got here

5. *go out*
   for three months

6. *leak*
   since last week

7. *live in Florida*
   since they retired

8. *snore*
   all night

9.

What Have They Been Doing?

(I have)	I've	
(We have)	We've	
(You have)	You've	
(They have)	They've	⟩ written.
(He has)	He's	
(She has)	She's	
(It has)	It's	

(I have)	I've	
(We have)	We've	
(You have)	You've	
(They have)	They've	⟩ been writing.
(He has)	He's	
(She has)	She's	
(It has)	It's	

A. Cynthia looks tired. What has she been doing?

B. She's been taking orders.

A. How many orders has she taken?

B. She's taken more than one hundred.

A. Wow! That's a lot of orders!

B. That's right. She's never taken that many orders before.

Ted

you

Amy and Rick

1. *give tennis lessons*
   more than 20

2. *write memos*
   more than 25

3. *assemble cell phones*
   at least 75

 Kevin

 Ms. Gomez

 you

4. *draw portraits*
around 30

5. *read resumes*
more than 200

6. *deliver packages*
over 50

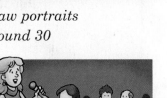 Jessica

 you and your brother

 Ron

7. *sing songs*
at least 40

8. *sell tee shirts*
well over 300

9. *do sit-ups*
at least 90

 Dr. Chin

 your children

 Jason

10. *see patients*
around 45

11. *build sandcastles*
10 or 11

12. *make smoothies*
more than 150

How to Say It!

Expressing Surprise

Wow! — That's incredible!
Gee! — That's amazing!
Boy! — That's unbelievable!
You're kidding! — I can't believe it!

Practice the conversations in this lesson again. Express surprise in different ways.

INTERVIEW   *How Long Have You . . . ?/How Long Did You . . . ?*

Interview another student. Then tell the class about the student you interviewed.

Where do you live now?
How long have you lived there?
Where did you live before?
How long did you live there?

Where do you (work/go to school) now?
How long have you (worked/gone to school) there?
Where did you (work/go to school) before?
How long did you (work/go to school) there?

9

They Had Done That Before

the day before

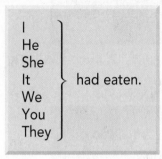

I
He
She
It
We
You
They
} had eaten.

A. Did Andrew eat lunch at Burger Town yesterday?

B. No. He didn't want to. He had eaten lunch at Burger Town the day before.

the weekend before

1. Did Sheila drive to the beach last weekend?

the night before

2. Did you go dancing last night?

the morning before

3. Did Paul make pancakes for breakfast yesterday morning?

the day before

4. Did your children have peanut butter and jelly sandwiches for lunch yesterday?

the evening before

5. Did you and your friends see a movie yesterday evening?

the Saturday before

6. Did the Browns take their children to the aquarium last Saturday afternoon?

It Had Already Begun

A. Did Alan get to the movie on time?

B. No, he didn't. By the time he got to the movie, it had already begun.

you

1. *plane*
   take off

Vicky

2. *bank*
   close

Mr. and Mrs. Slater

3. *play*
   start

you and your friends

4. *game*
   begin

Howard

5. *meeting*
   end

Emily

6. *train*
   leave the station

the Taylors

7. *ferry*
   sail away

Kathleen

8. *space launch*
   happen

Jerry

9. *graduation ceremony*
   finish

They Had Been Going Out for a Long Time

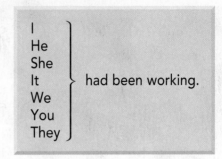

I	
He	
She	
It	had been working.
We	
You	
They	

A. Is it true that Dave and his girlfriend broke up?

B. Yes, it is.

A. I'm sorry to hear that. How long had they been going out?

B. They had been going out for a long time.

Is it true that . . .

1. you had to cancel your trip to Hawaii?
plan it

2. your husband got laid off at the factory?
work there

3. your grandparents had to sell their house?
live there

4. your daughter injured herself and couldn't participate in the gymnastics competition?
train for it

5. your son got sick and couldn't perform in the school play?
rehearse for it

6. you came down with the flu and you couldn't take the SAT test?
prepare for it

IT WASN'T THE WEDDING THEY HAD PLANNED

Albert and Helen Porter had worked very hard to prepare for their daughter Ashley's wedding last July. Ashley had always wanted to get married at home in an outdoor ceremony. Albert and Helen had spent months planning the wedding and getting their house ready for the celebration.

On the night before the wedding, as Albert and Helen went to sleep, they felt totally prepared for this special day. They had repainted the house. They had planted new flowers and bushes in the yard. They had even taken down the rusty old swing set that Ashley had played on as a child. They had rented a tent and a dance floor. They had set up tables and chairs. And they had hung decorations all around the yard.

However, when Albert and Helen woke up early on the morning of the wedding, they couldn't believe what had happened. There had been a big thunderstorm during the night. The tent had fallen down. The tables and chairs had tipped over. And all the decorations had blown away. And it was still raining!

Albert and Helen, not to mention Ashley, were extremely upset. But they quickly decided to move the celebration indoors. It wasn't the wedding they had planned, but it was still a wonderful day, and all their family and friends had a great time.

✔ READING *CHECK-UP*

TRUE, FALSE, OR MAYBE?

Answer True, False, or Maybe (if the answer isn't in the story.)

1. Ashley got married last spring.
2. She didn't want to get married indoors.
3. Ashley doesn't have any brothers or sisters.
4. The night before the wedding, Albert and Helen felt they had done everything to prepare for the wedding.
5. It had stopped raining by the time Albert and Helen woke up.

SIDE by SIDE JOURNAL

Sometimes we work hard to prepare for something—a test, a performance, a party, a special event, or something else. Sometimes things go well, and sometimes they don't. Write in your journal about something you had worked hard to prepare for. What was it? How long had you prepared for it? How had you prepared? What happened?

PRONUNCIATION   Reduced *have, has, & had*

Listen. Then say it.

How long have you been married?

How long has he owned this car?

How long had he been rehearsing for it?

Say it. Then listen.

How long have we been waiting?

How long has she been sick?

How long had they been living there?

GRAMMAR FOCUS

PRESENT PERFECT TENSE

(I have)	I've	
(We have)	We've	
(You have)	You've	
(They have)	They've	eaten.
(He has)	He's	
(She has)	She's	
(It has)	It's	

I		
We	haven't	
You		
They		eaten.
He		
She	hasn't	
It		

Have	I		
	we		
	you		
	they	eaten?	
Has	he		
	she		
	it		

Yes,	I		
	we	have.	
	you		
	they		
	he		
	she	has.	
	it		

No,	I		
	we	haven't.	
	you		
	they		
	he		
	she	hasn't.	
	it		

PRESENT PERFECT CONTINUOUS TENSE

(I have)	I've	
(We have)	We've	
(You have)	You've	
(They have)	They've	been working.
(He has)	He's	
(She has)	She's	
(It has)	It's	

PAST PERFECT TENSE

I	
He	
She	
It	had eaten.
We	
You	
They	

PAST PERFECT CONTINUOUS TENSE

I	
He	
She	
It	had been eating.
We	
You	
They	

Choose the correct answer.

1. I (went   have gone) to the bank an hour ago.

2. (He had   He's had) a cold since yesterday.

3. My roof is leaking. It (has   had) been leaking since last week.

4. We didn't want to see a movie last night. We (have   had) seen a movie the night before.

5. He (has   had) been writing memos since 9:00. He's already (been writing   written) more than fifty.

Perfect Modals:

Should Have
Might Have
May Have

Could Have
Must Have

- **Evaluating People's Activities**
- **Job Interviews**
- **Expressing Possibility**
- **Making Deductions**

- **Expressing Concern About Others**
- **Apologizing**
- **Recounting Difficult Situations**

VOCABULARY PREVIEW

1. answer the phone
2. apologize
3. daydream
4. fail
5. get lost
6. get stuck in *traffic*
7. hand over
8. oversleep
9. refuse
10. shake hands
11. skip *dessert*
12. yell

He Should Have Spoken Louder

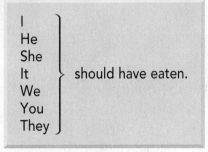

I	
He	
She	
It	should have eaten.
We	
You	
They	

A. Did Richard speak loud enough at the meeting this morning?

B. No, he didn't. He **should have spoken** louder.

1. Did Gail run fast enough during the marathon?

faster

2. Did Fred drive carefully enough during his driving test?

more carefully

3. Did Mr. and Mrs. Lopez get to the airport early enough?

earlier

4. Did you and your classmates study hard enough for the science quiz?

harder

5. Did Jason write legibly enough on his employment application?

more legibly

6. Did you take the cookies out of the oven soon enough?

sooner

7. Did Sally speak confidently enough at her job interview?

more confidently

8. Did Brian dance well enough at the audition?

better

She Shouldn't Have Driven to Work Today

Alice

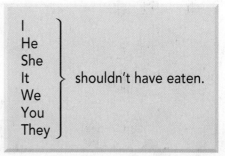

I
He
She
It
We
You
They
} shouldn't have eaten.

A. Why is Alice upset?

B. She thinks she **shouldn't have driven** to work today. She **should have taken** the train.

Carl

1. *buy a typewriter*
get a computer

Donna

2. *take Advanced French last semester*
take Beginning French

you

3. *cook vegetable stew for my guests*
make a salad

you and your wife

4. *see a movie last night*
stay home and watch TV

Michael

5. *wear jeans to a job interview today*
wear a suit

Mr. and Mrs. Parker

6. *go on a safari for their vacation*
go to the beach

Jennifer

7. *write her composition on the bus*
do it at home

Eric

8. *eat an entire cake for dessert*
have just one piece

THEY DIDN'T DO AS WELL AS THEY SHOULD HAVE

Barry didn't do as well as he should have at a job interview today. He didn't get the job, and he now realizes that he should have done a few things differently. He should have spoken more confidently, he should have told more about his previous experience, and he probably should have worn more conservative clothes.

In addition, he shouldn't have arrived late for his appointment. He shouldn't have asked questions only about vacations and sick days. And he DEFINITELY shouldn't have eaten his lunch in the interviewer's office. Barry will certainly do a few things differently the next time he has a job interview!

Vicky didn't do as well as she should have in a tennis tournament yesterday. She didn't win, and she now realizes that she should have done a few things differently. She should have practiced more during the week, she should have done more warm-up exercises before the tournament, and she probably should have gotten a good night's sleep the night before.

Furthermore, she shouldn't have used her old tennis racket. She shouldn't have eaten such a large breakfast that morning. And she DEFINITELY shouldn't have gone out dancing with her friends the night before. Vicky will certainly do a few things differently the next time she plays in a tennis tournament!

✔ READING CHECK-UP

TRUE, FALSE, OR MAYBE?

Answer True, False, or Maybe (if the answer isn't in the story).

1. Barry didn't speak confidently about himself at the interview.
2. He didn't get the job because he didn't have previous experience.
3. Barry likes to go on vacations and gets sick very often.
4. Vicky didn't get a good night's sleep the night before the tournament.
5. She used her old tennis racket during the tournament.
6. Vicky goes out dancing with her friends very often.

How About You?

Tell about a time when you didn't do as well as you should have. What was the situation? What should you have done differently?

LISTENING

Listen and choose the best answer based on the conversation you hear.

1. a. They should have gotten to the party earlier.
   b. They should have left later.

2. a. He should have spoken more softly.
   b. He shouldn't have spoken softly.

3. a. He should have dressed more comfortably.
   b. He should have spoken more confidently.

4. a. He should have studied harder.
   b. He should have written more legibly.

5. a. He shouldn't have left them in the oven.
   b. He shouldn't have taken them out of the oven.

6. a. She should have gotten a good night's sleep last night.
   b. She should have gotten up earlier this morning.

IN YOUR OWN WORDS

FOR WRITING AND DISCUSSION

What should you do if you want to do well at a job interview?

What should you talk about?
What should you ask about?
What should you wear?
What should you take with you?
When should you arrive?

(In your answers, use "You should . . .")*

* "You should" = "a person should."

She Might Have Gone to the Bank

I He She It We You They	might have may have eaten.

A. I wonder why Sheila hasn't come back from lunch yet.

B. I'm not sure. She { **might have** / **may have** } **gone** to the bank.

A. Hmm. Maybe you're right.

I wonder why . . .

1. Bob was late for the meeting
get stuck in traffic

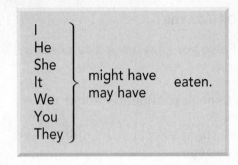

2. Professor Jones didn't come to class yesterday
be sick

3. Mr. and Mrs. Lane didn't come to our party
forget about it

4. Jimmy was late for school this morning
miss the bus

5. Peggy didn't want to go to the play with us
see it already

6. the neighbors haven't returned our ladder
break it

7. Dad left the rock concert early
have a headache

8. Grandma and Grandpa aren't answering their phone
go away for the weekend

READING

GEORGE HASN'T COME TO ENGLISH CLASS

George hasn't come to English class this evening, and all the students in the class are wondering why.

Henry thinks he might have gotten sick. Linda thinks he might have had a doctor's appointment. Mr. and Mrs. Kim think that one of George's children may have caught a bad cold. Carla thinks he may have had to work overtime. Mr. and Mrs. Sato think he might have gone to the airport to meet his relatives who are arriving from overseas. And Maria thinks he may have decided to study in another school.

All the students are curious about why George hasn't come to English class this evening . . . and they're a little concerned.

COMPLETE THE STORY

Complete this story about your English teacher. In your story, use names of students in your class.

Our English teacher hasn't come to class today, and all the students are wondering why.

_____ thinks _____.

_____ thinks _____.

_____.

_____.

_____.

And I think _____.

We're all curious about why our English teacher hasn't come to class today . . . and we're a little concerned.

He Could Have Gotten Lost!

Jack

| I |
| He |
| She |
| It |
| We |
| You |
| They |

} could have eaten.

A. If you ask me, Jack shouldn't have gone hiking by himself in the mountains.

B. You're right. He **could have gotten lost**!

Gloria

1. swim to the other side of the lake
drown

Billy

2. play baseball in the rain
catch a bad cold

Ann

3. ride her bicycle downtown during rush hour
get hurt

Jim

4. move his piano by himself
break his back

Jenny

5. use her computer during a thunderstorm
be electrocuted

your friends

6. go skating on the town pond
fall through the ice

Grandpa

7. shovel all the snow in the driveway
have a heart attack

Dad

8. argue with a police officer
wind* up in jail

9.

* wind–wound–wound

He Must Have Overslept

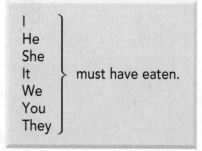

| I |
| He |
| She |
| It |
| We |
| You |
| They |

> must have eaten.

A. Richard came to work late today.

B. I'm really surprised to hear that. He NEVER comes to work late!

A. I know. He **must have overslept**.

B. You're probably right.

1. Maria missed English class all last week.
be very sick

2. Gary skipped dessert at the restaurant today.
go on a diet

3. Mrs. Grimsley smiled at her employees this morning.
be in a very good mood

4. Peter handed in his homework late this morning.
have a problem with his computer

5. Beverly yelled at me this morning.
be very upset

6. Walter was in a terrible mood today.
"get up on the wrong side of the bed"

7. You talked in your sleep last night.
have a bad dream

8. Rover refused to eat his dinner.
eat too many dog biscuits during the day

I'm a Little Concerned

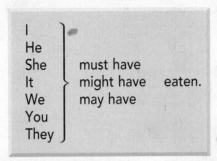

I
He
She
It
We
You
They
} must have
might have   eaten.
may have

A. Timmy looks frightened! He **must have seen a scary movie** today.

B. I'm not so sure. He { MIGHT **have** / MAY **have** } **seen a scary movie**, but that doesn't usually make him so frightened.

A. I'm a little concerned. Maybe we should talk to him.

B. That's a good idea.

A. Janet looks tired! She **must have worked overtime** today.

B. I'm not so sure. She { MIGHT **have** / MAY **have** } **worked overtime**, but that doesn't usually make her so tired.

A. I'm a little concerned. Maybe we should talk to her.

B. That's a good idea.

1. Mr. Jenkins looks exhausted!
   swim fifty laps

2. Rachel looks upset!
   fail an exam

3. Steve looks angry!
   have a fight with his landlord

4. Margaret looks tired!
   jog for a long time

5. Wayne looks upset!
   have an argument with the boss

6. Our English teacher looks disappointed!
   find a lot of mistakes in our homework

7. Rick looks exhausted!
   do a lot of sit-ups

8. Senator Wilson looks tired!
   shake* a lot of hands

* shake—shook—shaken

25

A. I want to apologize to you.

B. What for?

A. You must have been very angry with me yesterday.

B. I don't understand. Why should I have been angry with you?

A. Don't you remember? We had planned to **see a movie** yesterday, but I completely forgot!

B. Don't worry about it. Actually, I owe YOU an apology.

A. You do? Why?

B. I couldn't have **seen a movie** with you anyway. I had to **take care of my little sister** yesterday . . . and I completely forgot to tell you.

A. That's okay. Maybe we can **see a movie** some other time.

A. I want to apologize to you.

B. What for?

A. You must have been very angry with me yesterday.

B. I don't understand. Why should I have been angry with you?

A. Don't you remember? We had planned to _____ yesterday, but I completely forgot!

B. Don't worry about it. Actually, I owe YOU an apology.

A. You do? Why?

B. I couldn't have _____ with you anyway. I had to _____ yesterday . . . and I completely forgot to tell you.

A. That's okay. Maybe we can _____ some other time.

1. *go to the beach*
   study for my final exams

2. *have lunch*
   go to an important meeting

3. *take a walk in the park*
   visit a friend in the hospital

4.

How to Say It!

Apologizing

I want to apologize to you.

I need to apologize to you.

I owe you an apology.

I apologize.

I'm sorry.

Practice the conversations in this lesson again. Use different expressions for apologizing.

LUCKY PEOPLE

Gary must have been daydreaming while he was driving to work yesterday. He drove through a red light at the busiest intersection in town. Fortunately, he didn't hit anyone. Gary was lucky. He could have caused a terrible accident.

Mrs. Chen must have been very scared yesterday. There was a big, mean dog outside while she was putting out the garbage. Fortunately, the dog didn't see her. Mrs. Chen was lucky. That big, mean dog might have bitten her.

Howard must have been extremely irritable this morning. He was rude to his supervisor when she pointed out a mistake he had made. Fortunately, his supervisor was in a good mood, and she didn't get angry. Howard was lucky. His supervisor could have fired him.

Ms. Kendall must have been feeling very brave last night. She refused to hand over her purse to a man who was trying to mug her. Fortunately, the man got scared and ran away. Ms. Kendall was very lucky. She might have gotten hurt.

Mr. and Mrs. Gray must have had a lot of financial problems last year. They were never able to pay their rent on time. Fortunately, their landlord was very understanding. Mr. and Mrs. Gray are pretty lucky. Their landlord could have evicted them.

Irwin must have been very lonely yesterday. All evening he made long-distance phone calls to his friends throughout the country. Fortunately, most of his friends weren't home. Irwin was very lucky. He could have run up quite a big phone bill.

✓ READING CHECK-UP

TRUE, FALSE, OR MAYBE?

Answer True, False, or Maybe (if the answer isn't in the story).

1. Gary wasn't paying attention while he was driving to work.
2. Gary caused a terrible accident.
3. Mrs. Chen doesn't like dogs.
4. The dog didn't bite Mrs. Chen.
5. Howard was in a good mood yesterday.
6. Howard's supervisor is rarely in a bad mood.
7. Ms. Kendall didn't give her purse to the man.
8. Ms. Kendall had a lot of money in her purse.
9. Mr. and Mrs. Gray couldn't pay their rent on time last year.
10. The landlord evicted Mr. and Mrs. Gray.
11. Irwin's friends live throughout the country.
12. Irwin never communicates with his friends by e-mail.

WHICH WORD IS CORRECT?

1. Mr. and Mrs. Johnson didn't get to the train station on time. They (should have   must have) left their house earlier.
2. Alan was late for work today. He (should have   must have) overslept.
3. You're very lucky. You (could have   must have) gotten hurt.
4. I (may have   couldn't have) gone skiing with you anyway. I had to work.
5. Susan was an hour late for the meeting this morning. She (might have   should have) gotten stuck in traffic.
6. Arnold's cake tasted terrible! He (may have   should have) taken it out of the oven sooner.
7. I shouldn't have taken chemistry. I definitely (must have   should have) taken biology.
8. Janet wasn't paying attention. She (must have   should have) been daydreaming.
9. My cousin Ronald (shouldn't have   couldn't have) swum to the other side of the lake. He (must have   could have) drowned!
10. Roberta didn't come to the company picnic last Saturday. She (should have   may have) forgotten about it.

How About You?

Tell about a time when something bad *could have* happened to you, but didn't. What was the situation? What could have happened?

Tell about a time when you were
. . . lonely.
. . . scared.
. . . irritable.
. . . brave.

PRONUNCIATION Reduced *have*

Listen. Then say it.

He should have spoken louder.

She might have been sick.

They may have gone away.

Say it. Then listen.

You could have gotten hurt.

I must have overslept.

We shouldn't have gone there.

Write in your journal about a time when you did something and then you thought later that you should have done it differently. What did you do? What do you think you should have done?

GRAMMAR FOCUS

PERFECT MODALS:

SHOULD HAVE

I He She It We You They	**should have** eaten.

SHOULDN'T HAVE

I He She It We You They	**shouldn't have** eaten.

MUST HAVE

I He She It We You They	**must have** been upset.

MIGHT HAVE/MAY HAVE

I He She It We You They	**might have** **may have**	eaten.

COULD HAVE

I He She It We You They	**could have** gotten lost.

Choose the correct word.

1. Edward arrived a half-hour late for his job interview. He (must have   should have) gotten up earlier.

2. I'm surprised Carla missed the meeting this morning. She (should have   may have) gotten stuck in traffic.

3. Jack (shouldn't have   couldn't have) worn jeans to his interview. He (must have   should have) worn a suit.

4. Aunt Emma didn't come to the family picnic on Sunday. She (mustn't have   might have) been sick.

5. Marc (may have   shouldn't have) moved his sofa by himself. He (could have   mustn't have) hurt his back.

6. Paul almost got into an accident while he was driving today. He (must have   mustn't have) been daydreaming. He's lucky nothing happened. He (must have   may have) been badly hurt.

Passive Voice
Relative Pronouns

3

- Discussing Creative Works
- Describing Tasks Accomplished
- Discussing Things That Have Happened to People
- Describing Accomplishments
- Securing Services
- Automobile Repairs
- Historical Narratives
- Discussing Opinions

VOCABULARY PREVIEW

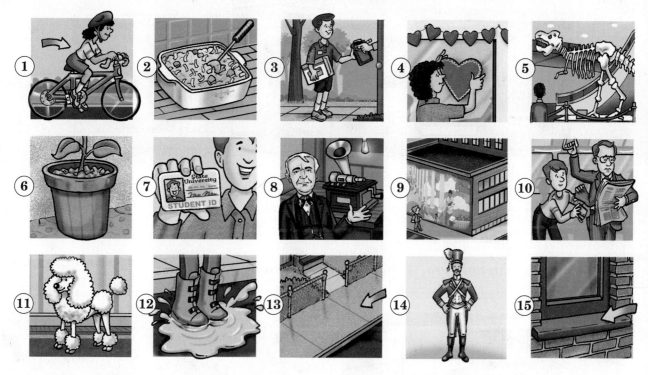

1. bicyclist	6. flowerpot	11. poodle
2. casserole	7. identification card	12. puddle
3. courier	8. invention	13. sidewalk
4. decorations	9. mural	14. uniform
5. dinosaur skeleton	10. pickpocket	15. windowsill

This Is a Very Scary Short Story!

Edgar Allan Poe wrote this short story.
This short story **was written** by Edgar Allan Poe.

A. This is a very scary short story!

B. I think so, too.

A. Who wrote it?

B. I'm not sure. I think it **was written** by Edgar Allan Poe.

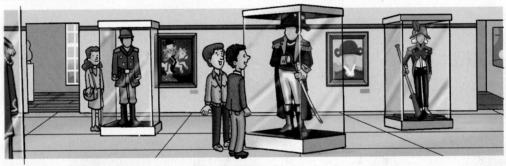

A. This is a very elegant uniform!

B. I think so, too.

A. Who wore it?

B. I'm not sure. I think it **was worn** by Napoleon.

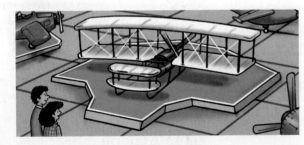

1. This is a very old airplane!
   fly • *the Wright Brothers*

2. This is a beautiful sonata!
   compose • *Mozart*

3. This is really a fascinating movie!
direct • *Fellini*

4. This is a very funny political cartoon!
draw • *Richard Hill*

5. This is a very interesting invention!
invent • *Thomas Edison*

6. This is a magnificent portrait!
paint • *Rembrandt*

7. This is an amazing dinosaur skeleton!
find • *archeologists in Asia*

8. This is an impressive building!
design • *Frank Lloyd Wright*

9. This is a very good photograph of you!
take • *Uncle George*

10. This is a very sad poem!
write • *Shakespeare*

11. This is an extremely colorful mural!
do • *the students at Central High School*

12. This is a delicious tuna casserole!
make • *Millie Swensen*

It's Already Been Written

> Somebody has written the report.
> The report **has been written**.
>
> Somebody has hung up the decorations.
> The decorations **have been hung up**.

A. Do you want me to write the accident report?

B. No. Don't worry about it. It's already **been written**.

A. Do you want me to hang up the decorations?

B. No. Don't worry about it. They've already **been hung up**.

1. *sweep the floor*

2. *do the dishes*

3. *set the alarm*

4. *set up the meeting room*

5. *give out the paychecks*

6. *distribute the mail*

7. *make the beds in Room 219*

8. *hide the teacher's birthday present*

9. *take out the trash*

10. *send the packages*

11. *feed the monkeys*

12. *sing the National Anthem*

Have You Heard About . . . ?

A. Have you heard about Helen?

B. No, I haven't. What happened?

A. She **was given** a raise last week.

B. That's great! That's the second time she's **been given** a raise this year!

A. Have you heard about Henry?

B. No, I haven't. What happened?

A. He **was hurt** during a football game last week.

B. That's terrible! That's the second time he's **been hurt** during a football game this year!

1. *Maria promoted*

2. *our mail carrier bitten by a dog*

3. *Aunt Martha invited to the White House*

4. *Stuart*
hit by a car

5. *Mr. and Mrs. Tyler*
robbed

6. *Jennifer*
offered a movie contract

7. *Frank*
fired

8. *Mrs. Mendoza*
taken to the hospital

9. *Arthur*
rejected by the army

10. *Diane*
sent to Honolulu on
business

11. *Albert*
chosen "Employee of the
Month"

12.

How to Say It!

Reacting to Good News

That's great!
That's fantastic!
That's wonderful!
That's great news!
That's fantastic news!
That's wonderful news!
I'm happy to hear that!
I'm glad to hear that!

Reacting to Bad News

That's terrible!
That's awful!
That's a shame!
That's a pity!
That's too bad!
What a shame!
What a pity!
How awful!
I'm sorry to hear that!

Practice the conversations in this lesson again. React to good and bad news in different ways.

READING

ALAN ALMOST DIDN'T GET TO WORK THIS MORNING

Alan almost didn't get to work this morning. As he was leaving his apartment building, he was hit on the head by a flowerpot that had just fallen from a windowsill. As he was walking to the bus stop, he was bitten by a dog, stung* by a bee, and splashed by a car that had just driven through a puddle. And while he was waiting for the bus, he was almost run over by a bicyclist who was riding on the sidewalk.

While he was riding on the bus, his wallet was stolen by a pickpocket who was standing behind him. All his money and identification cards were taken. As he was walking into his office building, he was accidentally knocked down by the courier who delivers the overnight mail. And when Alan finally arrived at work an hour late, he was yelled at by a manager who was in a very bad mood.

Poor Alan! What a way to begin the day!

* sting–stung–stung

✔ READING *CHECK-UP*

TRUE, FALSE, OR MAYBE?

Answer True, False, or Maybe (if the answer isn't in the story).

1. As Alan was leaving his apartment building, he was hit on the head by a windowsill.
2. As he was walking to the bus stop, a dog bit him, a bee stung him, and a car splashed him.
3. A bicyclist almost hit Alan.
4. Alan had a lot of money in his wallet.
5. Alan accidentally knocked down the courier who delivers the overnight mail.
6. Alan was yelled at because he wasn't on time for work.

How About You?

Have you ever had a bad day when everything went wrong? When? How did you feel? What happened?

 38

READING

A VERY EXCITING YEAR

In January Amelia was hired as a secretary by the Inter-Tel Company, which makes international telephone equipment. In March she was sent to school by the company to study statistics and information technology. In April she was given a raise. Just two months later, she was promoted to the position of supervisor of her department.

In August she was chosen "Employee of the Month," which is a great honor at Inter-Tel. In October she was given another raise. In November she was invited to apply for a position in the company's overseas office in Bangkok. And in December she was given the new job and was flown to Thailand to begin work.

Amelia certainly has had a very exciting year. She can't believe all the wonderful things that have happened to her since she was hired just twelve months ago.

✔ READING CHECK-UP

CHOOSE

1. The interviewer liked Amelia's resume, so she was given the _____.
   a. raise
   b. position

2. After Amelia had worked at the company for five months, she was _____.
   a. promoted
   b. hired

3. In August Amelia was _____ "Employee of the Month."
   a. chosen
   b. given

4. In December she was sent overseas _____ her company.
   a. as
   b. by

5. Over one hundred people had _____ the position in Bangkok.
   a. been invited to
   b. applied for

6. Many wonderful things have happened to Amelia since she was _____ twelve months ago.
   a. hired
   b. fired

How About You?

Tell about things that have happened to you during the past twelve months.

It's Being Repaired Right Now

Somebody is repairing my computer.
My computer is **being repaired**.

A. Hello. Is this Carol's Computer Repair Shop?

B. Yes, it is. Can I help you?

A. Yes, please. This is Mr. Lopez. I'm calling about my computer. Has it **been repaired** yet?

B. Not yet. It's **being repaired** right now.

A. I see. Tell me, when can I pick it up?

B. It'll be ready in about an hour.

A. Thank you.

A. Hello. Is this _____?

B. Yes, it is. Can I help you?

A. Yes, please. This is _____. I'm calling about my _____. (Has it / Have they) been _____ yet?

B. Not yet. (It's / They're) being _____ right now.

A. I see. Tell me, when can I pick (it / them) up?

B. (It'll / They'll) be ready in about an hour.

A. Thank you.

1. *Ms. Evans*
   VCR • fix

2. *Ted Clark*
   pants • take in

3. *Mrs. Withers*
   will • rewrite

4. *Glen Burns*
   poodle • clip

5. *Jennifer Wu*
   wedding cake • make

6.

READING

JOE'S AUTO REPAIR SHOP

Wilma Jones has been having a lot of trouble with her car recently, so she decided to take it to Joe's Auto Repair Shop to be fixed. The car is being repaired there right now, and it is receiving a LOT of attention from Joe and the other mechanics at his shop.

The engine is being tuned up. The oil is being changed. The battery is being charged. The brakes are being adjusted. The front bumper is being repaired. The broken headlight is being replaced. The hood is being repainted. The tires are being checked. And the broken rear window is being fixed.

Wilma is aware that she'll probably be charged a lot of money for these repairs. But she's confident that her car will be returned to her in excellent condition by the fine people who work at Joe's Auto Repair Shop.

✔ READING *CHECK-UP*

Q & A

Wilma Jones is calling Joe's Auto Repair Shop to find out about her car. Using this model, make questions and answers based on the story.

A. Have you *tuned up the engine* yet?
B. *It's* being *tuned up* right now.

LISTENING

Listen and choose the best line to continue the conversation.

1. a. Do you want me to send them?
    b. Who sent them?

2. a. Do you want me to make them?
    b. Who made them?

3. a. Was your cat hurt badly?
    b. Was your dog hurt badly?

4. a. Is she going to go?
    b. Is he going to go?

5. a. When will Mrs. Green begin working?
    b. When will Mr. Fleming begin working?

6. a. When will Mrs. Davis start her new job?
    b. When will Ms. Clark start her new job?

7. a. Oh, good. I'll pick it up in an hour.
    b. Oh, good. Call me when it's been fixed.

8. a. Oh, good. I'll pick it up right now.
    b. Oh, good. I'll pick it up when it's ready.

TALK ABOUT IT! *What's Your Opinion?*

Answers **should be written** in your notebook.
Students **should be required** to take an examination.
Camping **shouldn't be allowed** in public parks.

Talk about these issues with other students.

1. Should your native language be spoken during English class?

2. Should students be allowed to use dictionaries in class?

3. Should high school students be required to do community service?

4. Should young men and women be required to serve in the armed forces?

5. Should animals be used for medical research?

6. Should skateboarding be permitted on city streets and sidewalks?

7. Should camping be permitted in public parks?

8. Should children be allowed to see any movies they want to?

A NATIONAL HISTORIC LANDMARK

This building, which is the original headquarters of the Lord and Lady Department Store Company, was designed by the famous architect Archibald Morgan. It was built by the Vanderpool Construction Company. Construction was begun in 1845 and was completed in 1847. The building was officially opened in ceremonies that were held on April 13, 1847. These ceremonies were attended by the mayors of several cities, the governor, and the vice president of the United States.

The building's interior was destroyed by a fire that broke out in the early hours of the morning of February 3, 1895. After the fire, the building wasn't used for several years.

During World War I the structure was used as a warehouse for clothing and other materials that were sent to our soldiers overseas. After the war, the interior was rebuilt. Electric lights and modern plumbing were installed, and the Lord and Lady Department Store was officially reopened on June 17, 1921.

Since its opening day, the Lord and Lady Department Store has been considered one of the finest examples of nineteenth-century American architecture. The store has been visited by the presidents and prime ministers of many countries.

On December 5, 1973, this building was officially registered as a U.S. National Historic Landmark.

✔ READING CHECK-UP

WHAT'S THE ANSWER?

1. Who was the building designed by?
2. Who was the building built by?
3. When was construction begun?
4. When was it completed?
5. When was the building officially opened?
6. Who were the opening ceremonies attended by?
7. What happened on February 3, 1895?
8. What was the building used for during World War I?
9. When was the interior rebuilt?
10. When was the building reopened?
11. Since its opening day, what has the building been considered?
12. What happened on December 5, 1973?

CHOOSE

1. Cable TV service was _____ in my apartment this afternoon.
   a. opened
   b. installed

2. Our high school prom was _____ by all the students in our class.
   a. attended
   b. visited

3. The factory downtown was _____ by the fire.
   a. rebuilt
   b. destroyed

4. The construction has been completed, and now the store can be _____.
   a. rebuilt
   b. reopened

5. Our City Hall is _____ by many tourists because it's a very historic building.
   a. visited
   b. registered

6. Their wedding ceremony wasn't _____ outside because it rained.
   a. considered
   b. held

IN YOUR OWN WORDS

FOR WRITING AND DISCUSSION

Tell a story about the history of the place where you were born or a place where you have lived. You might want to use some of the following words in your story:

attacked	discovered
begun	founded
built	invaded
captured	liberated
closed	opened
conquered	rebuilt
destroyed	settled

PRONUNCIATION   Reduced Auxiliary Verbs

Listen. Then say it.

The engine is being tuned.

The brakes are being adjusted.

The store has been rebuilt.

Say it. Then listen.

The oil is being changed.

The tires are being checked.

The construction has been completed.

SIDE *by* **SIDE**
JOURNAL

Write in your journal about students' rights and responsibilities in your school. What are students required to do? What are they allowed to do? What are they not allowed to do?

GRAMMAR FOCUS

PASSIVE VOICE

This short story **was written** by Edgar Allan Poe.
The decorations **have been hung up**.
My computer **is being repaired**.

Students **should be required** to take an examination.
Camping **shouldn't be allowed** in public parks.

RELATIVE PRONOUNS

He was hit by a flowerpot **that** had just fallen.
He was knocked down by the courier **who** delivers the overnight mail.

She was hired by the Inter-Tel company, **which** makes international telephone equipment.

Choose the correct word.

1. I really like this photograph of you. I think (it's being   it was) taken by Dad.

2. You don't need to make the bed. It's already (was   been) made.

3. My wife just got a big promotion. It's the second time (she's been   she has) promoted this year.

4. The floor has (swept   been swept), the decorations have (hung up   been hung up), and the meeting room (is being   has) set up right now.

5. These are very funny cartoons. I think they (have   were) drawn by Richard Dawson.

6. The package to Honolulu has already (sent   been sent). It (has   was) sent this morning.

7. A truck almost (ran over   has been run over) a bicyclist on Main Street this morning.

8. The tires on your car (are   have) already (been   be) checked, and the mechanics are (being adjusted   adjusting) the brakes right now.

9. What's your opinion? Should students (allow   be allowed) to use dictionaries in English class?

10. The new museum was designed by the architect (who   which) had designed the public library.

11. After my accident, I was taken to a new hospital (who   that) had just opened the week before.

12. I was sent by my company on a business trip to Nairobi, (that   which) is the largest city in Kenya.

13. A. This is Ms. Chen. I'm calling about the computer (that   who) I brought in last week.

    B. Sorry. It hasn't (being   been) fixed yet. It's (being   been) fixed right now.

Feature Article
Fact File
Around the World
Interview
We've Got Mail!

SIDE by SIDE **Gazette**

Global Exchange
Listening
Fun with Idioms
What Are They
Saying?

Volume 4   Number 1

Inventions That Changed the World

Famous Inventions and Their Inventors

The first known antibiotic, penicillin, was discovered by Alexander Fleming in 1928. It was made from a mold called *penicillin*, which could kill bacteria. Since then, many other antibiotics have been discovered. Millions of lives have been saved by these antibiotics.

X-rays were discovered in 1895 by a German professor, Wilhelm Roentgen. People all over the world were amazed by his invention, the X-ray machine. This invention was so important that Roentgen was awarded the first Nobel Prize for Physics in 1901.

The screw was created over 2000 years ago. It was invented by a Greek named Archimedes. It was first used for watering fields. A person turned the giant wooden screw, which pulled water from lakes or rivers and sent it into fields. The water was used for irrigating crops. Much later, in the 1600s, screws were made by carpenters to hold things together. Today the screw is mass-produced and has an unlimited number of uses.

The telephone was invented by Alexander Graham Bell, a doctor and speech teacher for the deaf. The first phone call was made by Bell in 1876. He had spilled acid on his pants and wanted his assistant, Thomas Watson, to help him. The first words spoken on the telephone were "Mr. Watson, come here! I need you!"

Television was invented in 1926 by John Logie Baird, a Scottish inventor. Baird's television certainly didn't look like a television today! It was made out of a box, knitting needles, a cake tin, a bicycle lamp, and a cardboard disc. Electronic televisions like the ones we have today were invented by Vladimir Zworykin in the 1920s in the United States.

The first computer was built in 1946 by two American engineers, J. Presper Eckert, Jr., and John W. Mauchly. It was developed for the army, and it was so large that it took up an entire room! Later, in 1971, the "microchip" was invented, and small home computers were first produced for personal use. Today computers are involved in almost everything we do and are found almost everywhere we go.

FACT FILE

Time Line of Major Inventions

- **3500 B.C.:** the wheel invented
- **3000 B.C.:** toothpaste first used by Ancient Egyptians
- **2000 B.C.:** the sundial first used for telling time
- **1000 B.C.:** kites first flown in China
- **200 B.C.:** the screw invented in Greece for irrigation
- **105:** the first paper created by the Chinese
- **1200:** the abacus, a counting machine, introduced in China
- **1440:** the first printing press set up in Germany
- **1590:** the microscope invented
- **1791:** the first bicycle ridden in France
- **1876:** the telephone invented by Alexander Graham Bell
- **1895:** X-rays discovered by Wilhelm Roentgen
- **1903:** the first airplane flight made by Orville and Wilbur Wright
- **1908:** the first gas-powered cars assembled in the United States
- **1926:** the first television built by John Logie Baird in Scotland
- **1926:** penicillin discovered by Alexander Fleming
- **1946:** the world's first computer turned on
- **1961:** the first manned space flight launched by the Soviet Union
- **1977:** the first cell phones constructed by Bell Laboratory in New Jersey
- **1982:** compact discs introduced by Sony and Philips Corporations
- **1991:** the World Wide Web established

The wheel was invented about 3500 B.C. The first bicycle was ridden in France in 1791. When was the first microscope invented? What happened in 1876? Talk with other students about these major inventions.

Ancient and Modern Wonders of the World

The Pyramids were built as tombs for the kings of ancient Egypt more than 5000 years ago. They were constructed without machines and with very few tools. The kings were buried with many jewels, furniture, and personal treasures.

The Colosseum in Rome, Italy, was completed in 80 A.D. It was built as an amphitheater, a place for people to go to be entertained. Fights between gladiators, fights with beasts such as lions and tigers, and other battles were held there.

Machu Picchu was built high in the Andes Mountains of Peru by Incas during the period 1460 to 1470 A.D. Experts believe it was constructed for religious purposes. It was abandoned in the 1500s, but no one knows why.

Stonehenge is a group of huge stones that were erected in England during the period 2800 to 1800 B.C. No one knows who it was built by or why. Some people think it was used as a sundial to follow the position of the sun. Others think it might have been built as a temple for worshipping the sun.

The Taj Mahal in India was constructed by order of Shah Jahan in the 17th century. It was designed as a tomb for his favorite wife, who had died giving birth to their child. It was built by 20,000 men from many different countries. It is considered one of the most beautiful tombs in the world.

The Temple of Angkor Wat in Cambodia is one of the largest religious structures in the world. It was constructed in the 12th century and took about 30 years to build. The temple was dedicated to the Hindu god Vishnu. Today the site is being repaired and preserved by the United Nations and many countries.

The Great Wall of China was begun in the 3rd century B.C., and it wasn't completed until hundreds of years later. The wall was rebuilt, strengthened, and enlarged in the centuries that followed. It is estimated to be about 6000 kilometers in length. It is said that the Great Wall is even visible from the moon!

Tenochtitlan, an elaborate city in Mexico, was established in 1325 A.D. It was built on an island in the middle of a lake. According to legend, the Aztecs were told by an omen, or sign, to construct the city there. It was inhabited by 200,000 to 300,000 people. Mexico City is located on its ruins.

The Panama Canal was constructed in Panama to connect the Atlantic and Pacific Oceans. In 1901, the United States was given permission to build the canal. It was opened on August 15, 1914. The canal is used by more than 9000 ships a year, and it is maintained by approximately 8000 workers.

Which of these wonders would you like to visit? Why? What are some other wonders of the ancient or modern world that you know about?

Interview

A *Side by Side Gazette reporter recently interviewed international photojournalist Sam Turner. Sam has been taking news photographs for twenty years. His photos have been published in newspapers and magazines all over the world.*

Q: Sam, can you tell us a little about yourself?

A: Sure. Both my parents are American, but I was born in Sydney, Australia. My parents both worked for a big American bank, and they were transferred to Australia just before I was born. My parents and I spent a lot of time exploring Australia during our vacations. I was very influenced by those trips. I was really inspired by the natural beauty of the country.

Q: How did you first become interested in photography?

A: I was given a camera for my tenth birthday, and I took it along on a family trip to the Australian Outback. When I showed my photos to people, they were really impressed! I was encouraged to study photography.

Q: So did you go to photography school?

A: Yes, and I was chosen by my teachers as one of the most promising students in the school. One of my photos was selected for a national photo competition, and it won an award.

Q: What has been the most memorable event in your life?

A: I was invited by a group of mountain climbers to travel with them to Mt. Everest and take their photographs at the base camp at the bottom of the mountain. They were wonderful people, and it was a beautiful place.

Q: What photo have you been dreaming about taking someday?

A: I'd like to take a photo from the TOP of Mt. Everest! I'm not physically prepared for that right now, but someday I hope to make that journey. It's my dream!

FUN with IDIOMS

Do You Know These Expressions?

_____ 1. I was given the ax at work today.

_____ 2. Everybody was told about it, but I was left in the dark.

_____ 3. I was held up in traffic.

_____ 4. I was blown away by the mechanic's repair bill.

a. I was surprised.

b. I was stuck.

c. I was fired.

d. I didn't know.

We've Got Mail!

Dear Side by Side,

We are students in Ms. Baxter's class at the English Language School, and we have a question about the passive voice. It's very confusing for us. It requires different verb forms and different word order in the sentences. Why do we need it?

Sincerely,
"Actively Against the Passive"

Dear "Actively Against the Passive,"

Many students are confused by the passive voice. It is used very commonly in English, especially in written language such as textbooks and newspaper and magazine articles. The passive voice is often used when it isn't known or it isn't important who performs the action. For example:

The wheel was invented in 3500 B.C.
The school was built in 1975.
The paychecks have been given out.
The computer is being repaired.

When it is known or it is important who performs an action, the passive voice is sometimes used and is followed by a phrase that begins with the word "by." For example:

The telephone was invented by Alexander Graham Bell.
This novel was written by Alice Walker.

The passive voice is also used to focus attention on the subject of the passive sentence. For example:

The building was opened in 1847.
It was destroyed by a fire in 1895.
It was reopened in 1921.

So, even if you don't use the passive voice very much when you speak English, you will see it often in print, and you will also hear it being used. As time goes on, we're sure you'll feel more comfortable with the passive voice. Thanks for writing!

Sincerely,
Side by Side

Global Exchange

Kate1: Hi. Sorry I haven't been in touch recently. It's been a very busy time. I have some incredible news! Last month I was chosen "Outstanding Student of the Year" at my school. I was invited to a special ceremony at our city hall. During the ceremony, I was given a beautiful plaque to hang on my wall, and I was offered a college scholarship. The ceremony was attended by the mayor and lots of other important people in our city. My parents and my grandparents were there, and they were very proud. How have you been? What's new?

MarcJ: Hi. It's great to hear from you again. It's been a while. Congratulations on your award. I also have some news, but it isn't good news like yours. Two weeks ago I was hurt badly during a soccer game. I was taken to the hospital in an ambulance. The X–rays showed that my leg was broken in two places, so it was put in a cast. According to my doctor, I won't be allowed to play soccer for the rest of the season. As you can imagine, I'm very disappointed, but I'm confident I'll be back on the team next year. G2G* Talk to you soon.

Send a message to a keypal. Tell about some good or bad things that have happened to you recently.
*G2G = Got to go.

LISTENING NEWS REPORT

"News Report" True or False?

_____ ❶   **a.** A van was hit by a bicyclist.

_____ ❷   **b.** Joe Murphy lost the race for mayor.

_____ ❸   **c.** Five people were injured in the fire.

_____ ❹   **d.** The Terriers defeated the Eagles.

_____ ❺   **e.** The police discovered the robbery.

What Are They Saying?

Embedded Questions

- Asking for Information
- Indicating Uncertainty
- Referring People to Someone Else
- Reporting a Crime
- Reporting a Missing Person

VOCABULARY PREVIEW

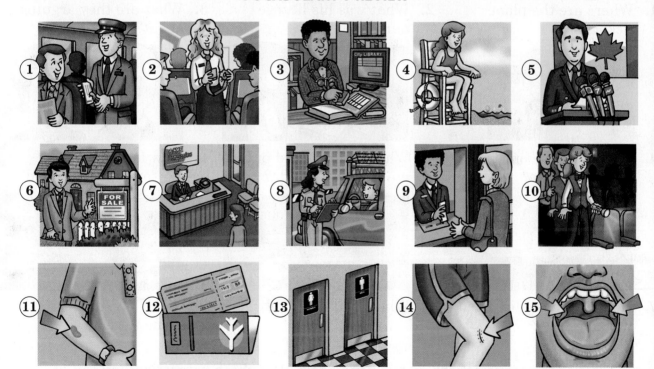

1. conductor
2. flight attendant
3. librarian
4. lifeguard
5. prime minister
6. real estate agent
7. receptionist
8. security guard
9. ticket agent
10. usher
11. birthmark
12. plane ticket
13. restrooms
14. scar
15. tonsils

I Don't Know Where the Cheese Is

Where is the bank?	I don't know where the bank is.
What is he doing?	I don't know what he's doing.
Why were they crying?	I don't know why they were crying.
When can he visit us?	I don't know when he can visit us.

A. Where is the cheese?

B. I don't know where the cheese is.

1. Where are the plane tickets?

2. What was his license number?

3. What are they arguing about?

4. When will the bus from Chicago arrive?

5. Who was the third prime minister of Canada?

6. How long have the Wilsons been married?

7. How long has Alice been working here?

8. Who should I vote for?

9. When is Santa Claus going to come?

Practice the conversations on this page again. Use these expressions instead of "I don't know."

I don't remember . . .   I'm not sure . . .
I can't remember . . .   I have no idea . . .
I've forgotten . . .

I Don't Know When the Movie Begins

Where does he live?	I don't know where he lives.
How often do they come here?	I don't know how often they come here.
How did she break her leg?	I don't know how she broke her leg.

A. When does the movie begin?

B. I don't know when the movie begins.

1. Where does Mr. Webster work?

2. How much do eggs cost this week?

3. Why did Richard get fired?

4. What time did the plane to Miami leave?

5. How often does the ice cream truck come by?

6. Where did Mom and Dad get married?

7. What does this word mean?

8. What did we do in class yesterday?

9. Why do young people like such loud music?

Practice the conversations on this page again. Use these expressions instead of "I don't know."

I don't remember . . .	I'm not sure . . .
I can't remember . . .	I have no idea . . .
I've forgotten . . .	

Do You Know What the Homework Assignment Is?

Where is the park?   Do you know where the park is?
When does the train leave?   Do you know when the train leaves?

A. Do you know what the homework assignment is?

B. I'm sorry. I don't know. You should ask Ronald.
HE can tell you what the homework assignment is.

A. Do you know how much this computer costs?

B. I'm sorry. I don't know. You should talk to that salesperson.
SHE can tell you how much this computer costs.

1. *ask that security guard*

2. *check with the ticket agent*

3. *ask Grandpa*

4. *talk to the boss*

5. *check with the mechanic*

6. *ask your sister*

7. *ask the people next door*

8. *talk with his supervisor*

9. *ask your nurse*

10.

How to Say It!

Asking for Information

Do you know
Can you tell me
Could you tell me
Could you please tell me } *what the homework*
Could you possibly tell me   *assignment is?*
Do you have any idea
Do you by any chance know

Practice the conversations in this lesson again. Ask for information in different ways.

ROSEMARY SMITH WAS ROBBED

Rosemary Smith was robbed about an hour ago while she was walking home from work. She's at the police station now, and she's having some trouble giving information to the police.

She knows that a man robbed her about an hour ago, but she simply can't remember any of the details. She doesn't know how tall the man was. She isn't sure how heavy he was. She can't remember what color hair he had. She has no idea what color eyes he had. She doesn't remember what he was wearing. She has forgotten what kind of car he was driving. She can't remember what color the car was. She has no idea what the license number was. And she doesn't even know how much money was taken!

Poor Rosemary! The police want to help her, but she can't remember any of the details.

✔ READING *CHECK-UP*

Q & A

You're the police officer. You're trying to get information from Rosemary Smith about the robbery. Using this model, make questions and answers based on the story.

A. Can you tell me* *how tall the man was*?
B. I'm sorry. I don't know *how tall he was*.

*Or: Do you know . . . ?	Do you have any idea . . . ?
Could you tell me . . . ?	Do you by any chance know . . . ?

CHOOSE

1. I'm not sure _____.
   a. where do they live
   b. where they live

2. She doesn't know _____.
   a. when the store opens
   b. when does the store open

3. Do you remember _____?
   a. where you put the car keys
   b. where did you put the car keys

4. Could you tell me _____?
   a. why is the boss angry
   b. why the boss is angry

5. I have no idea _____.
   a. how much they spent
   b. how much did they spend

6. He's forgotten _____.
   a. what is her name
   b. what her name is

A "SURPRISE" QUIZ

Mrs. Murphy is giving her students a "surprise" history quiz today, and Jeffrey isn't very happy about it. He has been absent for the past several days, and he's having a lot of trouble answering the questions.

He doesn't know who the nineteenth president of the United States was. He isn't sure when the Civil War ended. He doesn't remember when California became a state. He has forgotten where George Washington was born. He can't remember how many people signed the Declaration of Independence. He doesn't know where Abraham Lincoln was assassinated. He has forgotten why Washington, D.C. was chosen as the capital. And he has no idea what Alexander Graham Bell invented!

Jeffrey is very upset. He's sure he's going to fail Mrs. Murphy's "surprise" history quiz.

✔ READING *CHECK-UP*

Q & A

The history quiz is over, and Mrs. Murphy is going over the answers with her students. Using the story as a guide, complete the following conversation.

A. Who knows who the nineteenth president of the United States was?
B. I do. It was Rutherford B. Hayes.
A. And who can tell me _____?
C. I can. It ended in 1865.
A. Does anyone know _____?
D. Yes. It became a state in 1850.
A. Who remembers _____?
E. I remember. He was born in Virginia.
A. Can anybody tell me _____?
F. Yes. It was signed by 56 people.
A. Who knows _____?
G. He was assassinated at Ford's Theater in Washington, D.C.
A. And who can tell me _____?
H. It was chosen because the northern and southern states agreed it was a good location for the capital.
A. And finally, who remembers _____?
I. I do. He invented the telephone.
A. Very good, class!

57

Do You Know If Surfing Is Allowed at This Beach?

Is Tom in school today?

Do you know { if / whether } Tom is in school today?

I don't know { if / whether } Tom is in school today.

Does Mary work here?

Do you know { if / whether } Mary works here?

I don't know { if / whether } Mary works here.

Is surfing allowed at this beach?

A. Do you know { if / whether } surfing is allowed at this beach?

B. I'm not really sure. Why don't you ask the lifeguard?

SHE can tell you { if / whether } surfing is allowed at this beach.

Did anybody here find a cell phone?

A. Do you know { if / whether } anybody here found a cell phone?

B. I'm not really sure. Why don't you ask the cashier?

HE can tell you { if / whether } anybody here found a cell phone.

1. *Do you by any chance know . . . ?*
   ask Mr. Blake

2. *Could you please tell me . . . ?*
   ask the bus driver

3. *Can you tell me . . . ?*
   check with the librarian

4. *Do you know . . . ?*
   speak with Dr. Bell

5. *Do you by any chance know . . . ?*
   talk to our supervisor

6. *Do you have any idea . . . ?*
   ask the usher

7. *Do you know . . . ?*
   speak to the flight attendant

8. *Do you by any chance know . . . ?*
   check with the conductor

9. *Can you tell me . . . ?*
   ask those people over there

10.

READING

Thought bubbles:
- Did I break my arm? — **Frank**
- Have I lost too much weight? — **Mrs. Wilkins**
- Should I go on a diet? — **Arnold**
- Do my children have the measles? — **Mrs. Parker**
- Will I be able to play in the soccer match next week? — **Dan**
- Do I have to have my tonsils taken out? — **Linda**
- Do I need glasses? — **Edward**
- Am I pregnant? — **Vicki**

AT THE MIDTOWN MEDICAL CLINIC

It's a busy afternoon at the Midtown Medical Clinic. Lots of people are sitting in the waiting room and thinking about the questions they're going to ask the doctor.

Frank wants to know if he broke his arm. Mrs. Wilkins needs to know if she has lost too much weight. Arnold wants to find out whether he should go on a diet. Mrs. Parker is wondering whether her children have the measles. Dan is hoping to find out if he'll be able to play in the soccer match next week. Linda is going to ask the doctor whether she has to have her tonsils taken out. Edward expects to find out whether he needs glasses. And Vicki is anxious to know if she's pregnant.

Everybody is waiting patiently, but they hope they don't have to wait too long. They're all anxious to hear the answers to their questions.

✔ READING CHECK-UP

Q & A

The people in the story are registering with the receptionist at the Midtown Medical Clinic. Using this model, create dialogs based on the story.

A. I'd like to see the doctor, please.
B. What seems to be the problem?
A. I'm wondering (if/whether) *I broke my arm.*
B. All right. Please take a seat in the waiting room. The doctor will see you shortly.

CHOOSE

1. Do you know if ____?
   a. is it going to rain
   b. it's going to rain

2. I'm not really sure whether ____.
   a. the bus will be late
   b. will the bus be late

3. The teacher can tell us ____.
   a. if we'll have a test
   b. whether will we have a test

4. Can you tell me ____?
   a. whether have they moved
   b. whether they have moved

5. I'm anxious to know ____.
   a. how did I do on the exam
   b. how I did on the exam

6. Jackie is wondering ____.
   a. whether she got the job
   b. did she get the job

LISTENING

Listen and decide where the conversation is taking place.

1. a. a book store   b. a library   5. a. an airport   b. an airplane
2. a. a kitchen   b. a supermarket   6. a. a school   b. a doctor's office
3. a. a laundromat   b. a department store 7. a. a clinic   b. a hospital
4. a. a concert hall   b. a museum   8. a. a bus station   b. a bus stop

INTERACTIONS

Practice with another student. Read about each situation. Brainstorm more questions.
Then create a conversation, using the following expressions:

Do you know . . . ?	Could you please tell me . . . ?	Do you by any chance know . . . ?
Can you tell me . . . ?	Could you possibly tell me . . . ?	I'd like to know . . . .
Could you tell me . . . ?	Do you have any idea . . . ?	I'm wondering . . . .

Melinda wants to buy a house. She's visiting a house right now and talking with a real
estate agent.

How old is this house?
Does the roof leak?
_____ ?
_____ ?
_____ ?

Do you know how old this house is?
Can you tell me if the roof leaks?
_____
_____

Michael is planning to go to college next year. He's visiting a college right now and talking
with a person in the admissions office.

What courses do students
  have to take?
Does the school have a good
  library?
_____ ?
_____ ?
_____ ?

Could you please tell me what courses
  students have to take?
I'd like to know whether the school has
  a good library.
_____
_____
_____

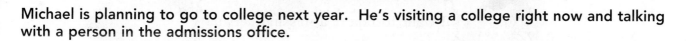

Police Department
Missing Person Information Sheet

1. What is your name?

2. What is the missing person's name?

3. What is his/her address?

4. How old is he/she?

5. How tall is he/she?

6. How much does he/she weigh?

7. Does this person have any scars, birthmarks, or other special characteristics?

8. Where was he/she the last time you saw him/her?

9. What was he/she wearing at that time?

10. What was he/she doing?

11. What is your relationship to the missing person?

12. What is your telephone number?

13. When can we reach you at that number?

A student in your class is missing! Call the police!

I want to report a missing person!

1.  Please tell me what your name is.

2.  And can you tell me what the missing person's name is?

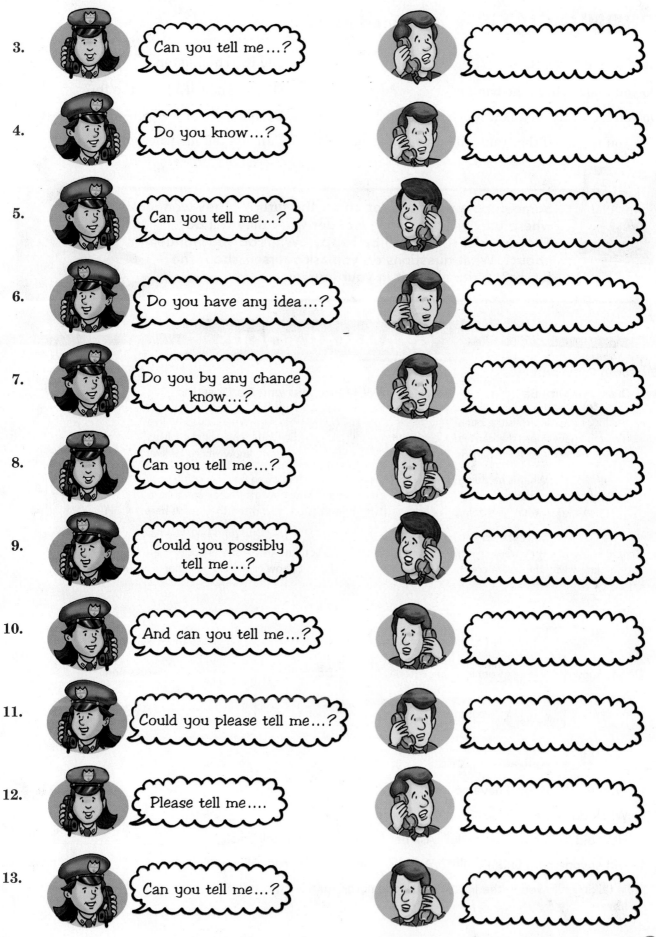

PRONUNCIATION   Reduced *you*

Listen. Then say it.

Do you know where the bank is?

Do you have any idea how much this costs?

Can you tell me if the train will arrive on time?

Say it. Then listen.

Do you know if I have the flu?

Do you have any idea if we're almost there?

Can you tell me whose dog this is?

Some people wonder a lot about the future. They wonder where they will live. They wonder what they will do. They wonder if they will be happy. What do **you** wonder about? What questions do you ask yourself about the future? Write about it in your journal.

GRAMMAR FOCUS

EMBEDDED QUESTIONS:

WH-QUESTIONS WITH BE

Where is the bank?
Do you know where the bank is?
I don't know where the bank is.

What is he doing?
Do you know what he's doing?
I don't know what he's doing.

Why were they crying?
Do you know why they were crying?
I don't know why they were crying.

WH-QUESTIONS WITH DO/DOES/DID

Where does he live?
Do you know where he lives?
I don't know where he lives.

How often do they come here?
Do you know how often they come here?
I don't know how often they come here.

How did she break her leg?
Do you know how she broke her leg?
I don't know how she broke her leg.

YES/NO QUESTIONS

Is Tom in school today?

Do you know { if / whether } Tom is in school today?

I don't know { if / whether } Tom is in school today.

Does Mary work here?

Do you know { if / whether } Mary works here?

I don't know { if / whether } Mary works here.

Complete the sentences.

1. Where's the dog? I have no idea _____ _____ _____ _____.

2. When does the train arrive? I'm not sure _____ _____ _____ _____.

3. How did Sally twist her ankle? Ask her brother. He can tell you _____ _____ _____ _____ _____.

4. Did anyone here find a wallet? Ask the manager. She can tell you _____ _____ _____ _____ a wallet.

5. Is talking allowed in the library? Ask the librarian. He can tell you _____ _____ _____ _____ in the library.

Conditional:
Present Real (If _____ Will)
Present Unreal (If _____ Would)

Hope-Clauses

- **Describing Plans and Intentions**
- **Consequences of Actions**
- **Discussing Future Events**
- **Expressing Hopes**
- **Asking for and Giving Reasons**
- **Making Deductions**
- **Emergencies**

VOCABULARY PREVIEW

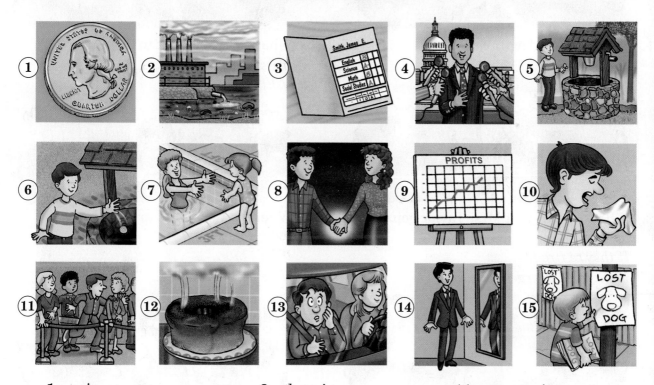

1. coin
2. pollution
3. report card
4. representative
5. wishing well
6. drop in
7. encourage
8. hold hands
9. increase
10. sneeze
11. aggressive
12. burnt
13. carsick
14. dressed up
15. missing

They Aren't Sure

| if _____ will _____ |

A. How is Angela going to get to work tomorrow?

B. She isn't sure.
If the weather is good, she'll probably ride her bicycle.
If the weather is bad, she'll probably take the bus.

1. What's Ben going to do this Saturday?
If it's sunny, ____.
If it rains, ____.

2. What are you going to do tomorrow?
If I still have a cold, ____.
If I feel better, ____.

3. What are Mr. and Mrs. Taylor going to do tonight?
If they're tired, ____.
If they feel energetic, ____.

4. Where is Roy going to have lunch today?
If he's busy, ____.
If he isn't busy, ____.

5. Where is Lisa going to go after school today?
If she has a lot of homework, ____.
If she doesn't have a lot of homework, ____.

6. What's Alan going to have for dessert this evening?
If he decides to stay on his diet, ____.
If he decides to forget about his diet, ____.

Do You Think . . . ?

if _____ might _____

A. Do you think Rover should come to the beach with us today?

B. No, I don't. If he comes to the beach with us today, he might get carsick.

1. Do you think Abigail should go to school today?

give her cold to the other children

2. Do you think I should skip my history class today?

miss something important

3. Do you think Roger should quit his job?

have trouble finding another one

4. Do you think I should put some more salt in the soup?

spoil it

5. Do you think we should try to break up that fight?

get hurt

6. Do you think Ricky should stay up and watch TV with us?

have trouble getting up in the morning

7. Do you think I should marry Norman?

regret it for the rest of your life

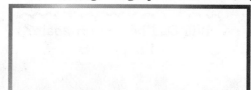

8.

67

I Hope Our Team Wins the Game Tomorrow

I hope it rains tomorrow.
I hope it doesn't rain tomorrow.

Will our team win the game tomorrow?
I hope so.

A. I hope our team wins the game tomorrow.

B. I hope so, too.

Will the teacher give a quiz today?
I hope not.

A. I hope the teacher doesn't give a quiz today.

B. I hope not, too.

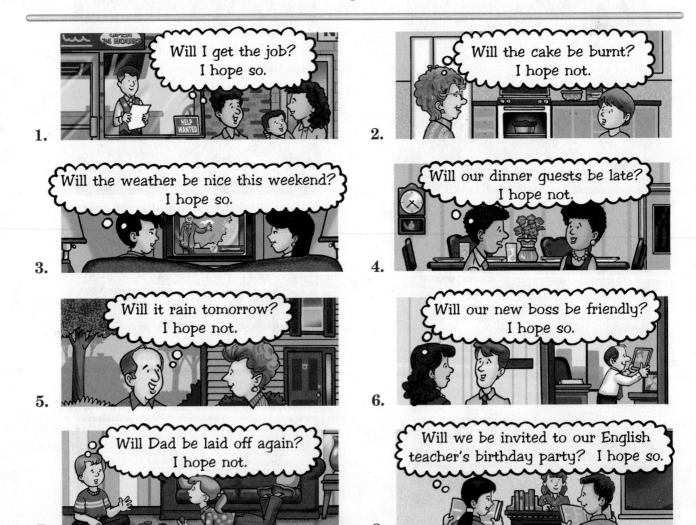

Will I get the job?
I hope so.

1.

Will the cake be burnt?
I hope not.

2.

Will the weather be nice this weekend?
I hope so.

3.

Will our dinner guests be late?
I hope not.

4.

Will it rain tomorrow?
I hope not.

5.

Will our new boss be friendly?
I hope so.

6.

Will Dad be laid off again?
I hope not.

7.

Will we be invited to our English teacher's birthday party? I hope so.

8.

I Hope

A. Do you think the train will be crowded?

B. I hope not.
If the train is crowded, we'll have to stand.
And if we have to stand, we'll be exhausted by the time we get to work!

A. You're right. I hope the train isn't crowded.

1.

A. Do you think the boss will retire this year?

B. I hope not.
If _____, his son will take his place.
And if _____, everybody will quit!

A. You're right. I hope _____.

2.

A. Do you think the economy will get worse this year?

B. I hope not.
If _____, I'll have to get a second job.
And if _____, my family will be very upset!

A. You're right. I hope _____.

3.

A. Do you think Mr. Mudge will increase our rent this year?

B. I hope not.
If _____, we won't be able to pay it.
And if _____, we'll have to move!

A. You're right. I hope _____.

4.

A. Do you think our computer will be at the repair shop for a long time?

B. I hope not.
If _____, we won't have access to the Internet.
And if _____, we won't be able to read our e-mail!

A. You're right. I hope _____.

THE WISHING WELL

There's a park in the center of Danville, and in the park there's a wishing well. It's a very popular spot with the people of Danville. Every day people pass by the wishing well, drop in a coin, and make a wish. Some people make wishes about their jobs, others make wishes about the weather, and lots of people make wishes about their families and friends.

Today is a particularly busy day at the wishing well. Many people are coming by and making wishes about their hopes for the future.

Ralph hopes he sells a lot of used cars this month. If he sells a lot of used cars, he'll receive a large year-end bonus.

Patricia hopes she gets a raise soon. If she gets a raise, her family will be able to take a vacation.

Andy hopes it snows tomorrow. If it snows, his school might be closed.

Nancy and Paul hope they find a cheap apartment soon. If they find a cheap apartment, they won't have to live with Paul's parents anymore.

Claudia hopes her next movie is a big success. If it's a big success, she'll be rich and famous.

John hopes he gets good grades on his next report card. If he gets good grades, his parents will buy him the CD player he has wanted for a long time.

Mr. and Mrs. Clark hope they live to be a hundred. If they live to be a hundred, they'll be able to watch their grandchildren and great-grandchildren grow up.

J.P. Morgan hopes the nation's economy improves next year. If the economy improves, his company's profits will increase.

And Wendy hopes she gets accepted to medical school. If she gets accepted to medical school, she'll become a doctor, just like her mother and grandfather.

You can see why the wishing well is a very popular spot with the people of Danville. Day after day, people pass by, drop in their coins, and hope that their wishes come true.

✔ READING *CHECK-UP*

Q & A

You're talking with the people in the story. Using this model, create dialogs based on the story.

A. I hope *I sell a lot of used cars this month*.
B. Oh?
A. Yes. If *I sell a lot of used cars, I'll receive a large year-end bonus*.
B. Well, good luck! I hope *you sell a lot of used cars*!
A. Thanks.

CHOOSE

1. We hope our landlord doesn't _____ our rent.
   a. increase
   b. improve

2. Jennifer is very smart. She gets good _____ in all her subjects.
   a. cards
   b. grades

3. People go to the wishing well and make _____ about the future.
   a. profits
   b. wishes

4. Have you _____ today's mail yet?
   a. received
   b. accepted

5. Arthur hopes his new Broadway play is a big _____.
   a. access
   b. success

6. The company couldn't increase my salary this year, but they gave me a very nice _____.
   a. raise
   b. bonus

If They Lived Closer, They'd Visit Us More Often

if _____ would _____

(I would)	I'd	
(He would)	He'd	
(She would)	She'd	
It would		work.
(We would)	We'd	
(You would)	You'd	
(They would)	They'd	

A. Why don't our grandchildren visit us more often?

B. They don't live close enough.
If they lived closer, they'd visit us more often.

A. Why isn't Alexander able to lift weights?

B. He isn't strong enough.
If he were* stronger, he'd be able to lift weights.

* If [I, he, she, it, we, you, they] were . . .

1. Why don't I feel energetic?
You don't sleep enough.
If _____.

2. Why isn't Sally a good driver?
She isn't careful enough.
If _____.

3. Why doesn't Brian get good grades?

He doesn't study enough.

If _____.

4. Why aren't you satisfied with your job?

I don't get paid enough.

If _____.

5. Why doesn't Amy have friends at school?

She isn't outgoing enough.

If _____.

6. Why doesn't Stan have a yearly checkup?

He doesn't care enough about his health.

If _____.

7. Why aren't most Americans in good physical condition?

They don't exercise enough.

If _____.

8. Why isn't Melvin a good salesman?

He isn't aggressive enough.

If _____.

9. Why doesn't my car get better gas mileage?

You don't tune up your engine often enough.

If _____.

10. Why don't you and Janet get along with each other?

We don't have enough in common.

If _____.

11. Why don't our representatives in Congress do something about pollution?

They aren't concerned enough about the environment.

If _____.

12. Why doesn't our English teacher buy a new pair of shoes?

He doesn't make enough money.

If _____.

73

If She Didn't Like Her Job, She Wouldn't Work So Hard

if _____ wouldn't (would not) _____

A. I wonder why Olivia works so hard.

B. She must like her job.

A. You're probably right.
If she didn't like her job, she wouldn't work so hard.

A. I wonder why Paul is so dressed up.

B. He must have a job interview.

A. You're probably right.
If he didn't have a job interview, he wouldn't be so dressed up.

1. I wonder why Gary is so nervous.
He must have an exam today.

2. I wonder why our supervisor is shouting at us today.
She must be in a bad mood.

3. I wonder why Rover is barking at the door.
He must want to go outside.

4. I wonder why Melanie wants to be a schoolteacher.
She must like children.

5. I wonder why Gregory makes so many mistakes.
He must be careless.

6. I wonder why Beth is home tonight.
She must have to take care of her little brother.

7. I wonder why Donald gets into so many fights.
He must like to argue with people.

8. I wonder why my brother and his girlfriend hold hands all the time.
They must be in love.

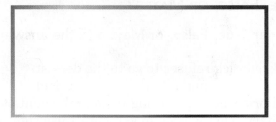

9. I wonder why I'm sneezing so much.
You must be allergic to my perfume.

10.

75

READING

THEY WOULD BE WILLING TO IF . . .

For several months, Frederick has been pressuring his wife, Doris, to go to the dentist, but she refuses to go. The reason is that she can't stand the sound of the dentist's drill. Doris says that if the dentist's drill didn't bother her so much, she would be willing to go to the dentist. Frederick hopes his wife changes her mind and goes to the dentist soon.

For several months, Barry's family has been encouraging him to ask his boss for a raise, but Barry refuses to do it. The reason is that he's afraid his boss might get angry and say "No." Barry says that if he weren't afraid of his boss's reaction, he would be willing to ask for a raise. Barry's family hopes he changes his mind and asks for a raise soon.

✔ READING CHECK-UP

TRUE, FALSE, OR MAYBE?

Answer True, False, or Maybe (if the answer isn't in the story).

1. Frederick refuses to go to the dentist.
2. Doris is going to find a different dentist.
3. Doris would be willing to go to the dentist if the sound of the drill didn't bother her.
4. Barry isn't willing to ask for a raise right now.
5. If Barry asked for a raise, his boss would say "No."
6. Barry's family began to encourage him to ask for a raise one month ago.

LISTENING

Listen and choose the statement that is true based on what you hear.

1. a. It's raining today.
   b. It isn't raining today.

2. a. We have enough money.
   b. We don't have enough money.

3. a. Mrs. Carter isn't her English teacher.
   b. Mrs. Carter is her English teacher.

4. a. They might receive bonuses.
   b. The company's profits didn't increase.

5. a. He isn't allergic to trees.
   b. He isn't going hiking this weekend.

6. a. He isn't going to the movies tonight.
   b. He doesn't have to work tonight.

TALK ABOUT IT! *Are You Prepared for Emergencies?*

Talk with other students about these emergencies.

1. What would you do if you saw a bad accident?

2. What would you do if you saw someone having a heart attack?

3. What would you do if somebody in your family were missing?

4. What would you do if you were bitten by a dog?

5. What would you do if you were at the beach and you saw someone drowning?

6. What would you do if somebody came up to you on the street and tried to rob you?

7. What would you do if a fire broke out in your house or apartment?

8. What would you do if you were lying in bed and you heard someone trying to break into your house or apartment?

Think of some other emergencies and talk with other students about what you would do.

SIDE by SIDE JOURNAL

What would you do with the money if you won a million dollars on a TV game show? Write about it in your journal.

Listen. Then say it.

If I got paid more, I'd be satisfied with my job.

If she were more outgoing, she'd have friends
at school.

Say it. Then listen.

If we had more in common, we'd get along better.

If you tuned up your car more often, it'd get
better gas mileage.

GRAMMAR FOCUS

PRESENT REAL CONDITIONAL (IF ___ WILL)

If	I / we / you / they	feel	better,	I'll / we'll / you'll / they'll	eat dinner.
	he / she / it	feels		he'll / she'll / it'll	

PRESENT UNREAL CONDITIONAL (IF ___ WOULD)

If	I / he / she / we / you / they	had more time,	I'd / he'd / she'd / we'd / you'd / they'd	study more.

If	I / he / she / we / you / they	didn't have an exam,	I / he / she / we / you / they	**wouldn't** be nervous.

If	I / he / she / we / you / they	were stronger,	I'd / he'd / she'd / we'd / you'd / they'd	be able to do that.

If	I / he / she / we / you / they	weren't careless,	I / he / she / we / you / they	**wouldn't** make mistakes.

HOPE-CLAUSES

I / We / You / They	hope	I / we / you / they	get	a raise soon.
He / She	hopes	he / she	gets	

I hope it rains tomorrow.
I hope it doesn't rain tomorrow.

I hope the weather is nice this weekend.
I hope the weather isn't bad this weekend.

Complete the sentences.

1. Alan doesn't get good grades because he doesn't study enough. If _____ _____ more, _____ get
   good grades.

2. I'm not a good dancer because I'm not graceful. If _____ _____ graceful, _____ _____ a good dancer.

3. Alexandra is nervous today. She must have a big exam. If _____ _____ _____ a big exam,
   _____ _____ _____ nervous.

4. I hope the bus _____ on time today. If _____ _____ on time, _____ get to work late.
   And if _____ _____ to work late, my supervisor _____ _____ angry.

Feature Article
Fact File
Around the World
Interview
We've Got Mail!

Global Exchange
Listening
Fun with Idioms
What Are They
Saying?

Volume 4   Number 2

The Music of Wishes and Hopes

Songwriters often express wishes and hopes through their music. Their songs are filled with lyrics such as "If I could . . . ," "If I had . . . ," "If I were. . . ," I wish . . . ," and "I hope . . . ." Here are some favorite songs about wishes and hopes from the worlds of popular, folk, Broadway, country, and rock music.

"If I Had a Hammer": This famous folk song was originally written as a poem by Lee Hays, then put to music by Pete Seeger. The singer sings about what he would do to bring peace all over the land. He sings that if he had a hammer, he'd hammer in the morning. If he had a bell, he'd ring it. If he had a song, he'd sing it. This popular tune was made famous by the folk singers Peter, Paul, and Mary.

"(If I Could Save) Time in a Bottle": In this song written by Jim Croce, the singer wishes he had more time to spend with his girlfriend. If it were possible, he would save time the way people save money. He would save the days in a bottle and then spend all the time with the one he loves.

"If I Had a Million Dollars": In this popular song sung by the Canadian group Barenaked Ladies, the leader of the group sings about what he would do if he had a million dollars. He would buy the woman he loves a house, furniture, a car, an exotic pet, a green dress, and other things.

"I Hope You Dance": This song of hope is sung by the popular country music singer Lee Ann Womack. She sings about her hopes for the people she loves. She hopes they never go hungry or without love. She hopes they find joy in simple pleasures like the ocean. She hopes they appreciate what they have.

"If I Were a Bell": In this song from the musical *Guys and Dolls*, Sarah Brown sings about her feelings for the man she loves, a gambler named Sky Masterson. She is so happy that if she were a bell, she'd be ringing. If she were a gate, she'd be swinging.

"If I Were a Rich Man": In the musical *Fiddler on the Roof*, Tevye, a poor dairyman, sings that he wishes he were rich. If he were a rich man, he wouldn't have to work hard, and he would build a big house for his family.

"(If I Could) Change the World": Singer Eric Clapton won a Grammy Award for this song from the movie *Phenomenon*. In this song, the singer wishes he could change the world and be with the girl he loves. If he could, he would be the center of her universe. He would be a king, and she would be a queen. But for now, he realizes it's impossible.

Try to find some of these songs and listen to them. Do you know other songs about wishes and hopes?

FACT FILE

Song Search

WORD	NUMBER OF SONGS WITH WORD IN TITLE
"if"	1130
"hope"	41
"wish"	149

Making Wishes

There are many different traditions and customs for making wishes around the world.

If you find a four-leaf clover, make a wish and then throw the clover away. (Ireland)

When you see a new moon, hold a coin up to the moon and wish for money. As the moon increases, your money will increase. (Jamaica)

If you make a wish as you throw a coin or a pebble into a wishing well, your wish may come true. (Many countries)

Make a wish before you blow out the candles on a birthday cake. (The United States and other countries)

If you open a nutshell and find two nuts instead of one, give one to a friend. Each of you should make a wish. If you're the person who remembers to say "lucky nut" the next morning, you will get your wish. (Russia)

At midnight on New Year's Eve, eat one grape for each of the twelve chimes of the clock. Make the same wish as you eat each grape and your wish will come true. (Spain, Portugal, and Venezuela)

If you catch a falling leaf, make a wish. (Japan)

When you see lightning, make a wish. (The Philippines)

Hold one end of a wishbone (from a chicken or turkey) while someone else holds the other end. Make a wish, then break the wishbone. If you get the longer piece, your wish will come true. (The United States)

When you see the first full moon of the year, make a wish. (Korea)

Stand with your back to a fountain. Throw three coins, one at a time, over your shoulder into the water. Each time make the same wish. If you hear the coins splash into the water three times, your wish will come true. (Europe)

When you see the first star in the evening sky, say this poem and make a wish:

Star light, star bright,
First star I see tonight.
I wish I may, I wish I might
Have the wish I wish tonight.

(Many countries with similar poems in different languages)

Which of these traditions for wishing did you know about? What are some traditions that you know?

Interview

**A Side by Side Gazette
*reporter asked these people:***

Q. What would you do if you won a million dollars?

A. I'd pay all my bills, and I'd pay off all my debts. I'd put the rest of the money in the bank.

A. I think I would quit my job and travel around the world.

A. I'd invest some money, and I'd save the rest for my children's college education.

A. I don't know. I wouldn't quit my job, that's for sure! I wouldn't know what to do if I had so much free time.

A. I'd help my parents. They don't have a lot of money. I'd buy them a house in a nice neighborhood.

A. I'd give most of the money to charities that help people. I'd really feel good if I could do that.

A. All my life I've dreamed about starting my own business. I'd open up a flower shop, and my dream would come true.

FUN with IDIOMS

Do You Know These Expressions?

_____ 1. You're breaking my heart.

_____ 2. You light up my life.

_____ 3. You're a heel!

_____ 4. You've got me wrapped around your little finger.

a. I'm very happy.

b. I'll do anything for you.

c. I'm very sad.

d. You aren't a nice person.

Dear Side by Side,

I'm confused about the correct tense to use with the word "hope." It seems to me that the future tense should be used when someone expresses hope about the future. For example, I think a person should say, "I hope the weather will be nice tomorrow." But according to my teacher, the present tense should be used: "I hope the weather is nice tomorrow." And I'm sure I've heard English speakers use the future tense after the word "hope." Are these people making a grammar mistake?

Sincerely,

"Hoping for an Answer"

Dear "Hoping for an Answer,"

Yes, those people are making a very common grammar mistake. We understand why you think the future tense should be used to express hope about the future. It seems to make sense. Unfortunately, grammar rules in English don't always make sense! In this case, the rule is that the present tense should be used. We hope this answers your question.

Sincerely,

Side by Side

Dear Side by Side,

I have a question about the words "were" and "was" in conditional sentences. According to your book, the following sentences are correct:

If he **were** stronger, he'd be able to lift weights.

If I **were** bitten by a dog, I'd call the doctor.

If she **weren't** in a bad mood, she wouldn't be shouting.

But I think it's better to use the word "was" instead of "were" in these sentences. Plus, I hear people use "was" in sentences like these all the time! Can you explain this?

Sincerely,

"Confused About Conditionals"

Dear "Confused About Conditionals,"

Your question is wonderful because it shows the difference between grammatically correct English and the informal English people use every day. "Were" is the grammatically correct verb in these conditional sentences. However, it is indeed very common in informal speech for people to say "was." If you were a student in our classroom, we would encourage you to use "were." That's the correct form, and after all, you're studying the rules of the language!

Sincerely,

Side by Side

Sari4: Hi! It's Friday afternoon, and I just got home from school. I'm really looking forward to the weekend. I'm not sure yet what I'm going to do. If the weather is nice tomorrow, I might go bicycling with some friends. If the weather is bad, we might go bowling or see a movie. On Sunday, if my cousins from Toronto visit us, my family will probably make a big dinner at home. If they don't visit, we'll probably have a picnic in the park. What are YOUR plans for the weekend?

Send a message to a keypal. Tell about your plans for the weekend.

LISTENING

Tempo Airlines

Press

_e_	❶	**a.**	to plan a vacation
___	❷	**b.**	to repeat the menu
___	❸	**c.**	to fly in the U.S. or Canada
___	❹	**d.**	to speak to a representative
___	❺	**e.**	to find out about today's flights
___	❻	**f.**	to fly overseas
___	❼	**g.**	to get travel awards
___	❽	**h.**	to listen to airport check-in rules

What Are They Saying?

Present Unreal Conditional (continued)
Wish-Clauses

- Advice
- Expressing Wishes
- Job Satisfaction
- Expressing Ability
- Asking for and Giving Reasons
- Life in Cities and Suburbs

VOCABULARY PREVIEW

1. classified ad
2. day shift
3. night shift
4. full-time job
5. part-time job

6. baby food
7. baby picture
8. beard
9. driver's ed
10. fan

11. foreign language
12. obituary
13. pronunciation
14. taxes
15. voter

If I Were You

A. Do you think the boss would be angry if I went home early?

B. Yes, I do. I think she'd be VERY angry.

A. Do you really think so?

B. Yes. I'm positive. I wouldn't go home early if I were you.

A. I suppose you're right.

1. Do you think Ted would be disappointed if I missed his birthday party?

2. Do you think Mom would be angry if I drove her new car?

3. Do you think the neighbors would be annoyed if I practiced the drums now?

4. Do you think Mrs. Riley would be upset if I skipped English class tomorrow?

5. Do you think the owners of the building would be upset if I painted the kitchen purple?

6. Do you think my parents would be disappointed if I dropped out of medical school?

7. Do you think Roy would be jealous if I went out with his girlfriend?

8. Do you think Dad would be mad if I borrowed his cell phone?

9. Do you think the voters would be upset if I raised taxes?

10. Do you think my fans would be unhappy if I got a haircut?

11. Do you think Matt would be embarrassed if I showed his baby pictures to his girlfriend?

12.

To Tell the Truth

A. I'm thinking of **growing a beard**. What do you think?

B. To tell the truth, I wouldn't **grow a beard** if I were you.

A. Why do you say that?

B. If you **grew a beard**, you'd probably **look very funny**.

A. Hmm. You might be right.

1. *buy a used car from Ralph Jones*
spend a lot of money on repairs

2. *get a dog*
be evicted from your apartment building

3. *start an Internet company*
"lose your shirt"

4.

How to Say It!

Giving a Personal Opinion

To tell the truth,
To tell you the truth,
To be honest,
To be honest with you,
If you ask me,
} *I wouldn't grow a beard.*

Practice the conversations on this page again. Use different expressions for giving a personal opinion.

Wishes

Tom **lives** in Boston.   He **wishes** he **lived** in New York.

A. Do you enjoy driving a taxi?

B. Not really. I wish I drove a school bus.

A. Does Mr. Miller enjoy being a teacher?

B. Not really. He wishes he were an actor.

1. Does Alice enjoy living in the suburbs?
   in the city

2. Does Barry enjoy being single?
   married

3. Does Mrs. Dexter enjoy teaching music?
   something else

4. Do you enjoy working the night shift?
   the day shift

5. Does Vincent enjoy painting houses?
   portraits

6. Does Ann enjoy having two part-time jobs?
   one good full-time job

7. Do you enjoy being the vice president?
   the president

8. Does Albert enjoy having a cat?
   a dog

9.

"SICK AND TIRED"

Frank is "sick and tired" of selling used cars! He has been doing that for twenty-eight years. Frank wishes he sold something else. In fact, at this point in his life, he would be willing to sell ANYTHING as long as it wasn't used cars!

Peggy is "sick and tired" of writing classified ads and obituaries for the Midville Times! She has been doing that since 1989. Peggy wishes she wrote something else. In fact, at this point in her life, she'd be willing to write ANYTHING as long as it wasn't classified ads and obituaries!

Mr. Dellasandro is "sick and tired" of teaching driver's ed! He has been teaching that for the past twenty-one years. "Mr. D" wishes he taught something else. In fact, at this point in his life, he would be willing to teach ANYTHING as long as it wasn't driver's ed!

Patty and Jimmy are "sick and tired" of eating tuna fish sandwiches for lunch. They have been eating them for lunch every day for the past four years. Patty and Jimmy wish their parents would give them something else for lunch. In fact, at this point in their lives, they would be willing to eat ANYTHING for lunch as long as it wasn't tuna fish sandwiches!

✓ READING *CHECK-UP*

CHOOSE

1. Tom found his job through the _____.
   a. classified ads
   b. obituaries

2. If you don't visit Aunt Nellie in the hospital, she'll be very _____.
   a. disappointed
   b. sick and tired

3. I was _____ when my driver's ed teacher shouted at me in front of the other students.
   a. jealous
   b. embarrassed

4. I enjoy working the _____.
   a. night shift
   b. full time

5. Howard _____ the meeting because he had to go to the dentist.
   a. dropped out of
   b. skipped

6. This is a _____ of me that was painted when I was three years old.
   a. portrait
   b. photograph

They Wish They Could

A. Can Jeffrey cook?

B. No, he can't . . . but he wishes he could. If he could cook, he'd **invite his friends over for dinner**.

1. Can Brian dance?
go dancing every night

2. Can Cheryl type fast?
be able to leave work on time

3. Can Steve speak a foreign language?
be able to get a better job

4. Can Martha knit?
make sweaters for her grandchildren

5. Can Gary fix his car by himself?
save a lot of money

6. Can Mr. and Mrs. Bradley ski?
take their children skiing in Colorado

7. Can Abby play a musical instrument?
be able to march in the town parade

8. Can Jessica talk?
tell her parents she doesn't like her baby food

9. Can Richard roll his "Rs"?
have better pronunciation in Spanish

10.

89

Why Do You Say That?

My TV is fixed. ☹

A. You know, I wish my TV weren't fixed.

B. Why do you say that?

A. If it weren't fixed, { I could / I'd be able to } talk with my children.

My son wants to be a dentist. ☹

A. You know, I wish my son didn't want to be a dentist.

B. Why do you say that?

A. If he didn't want to be a dentist, { I could / I'd be able to } convince him

to manage my shoe store when I retire.

1. *wear my new raincoat this Saturday*

2. *go to the beach*

3. *have a garden*

4. *see her more often*

5. *concentrate more on my work*

6. *go away for the weekend*

7. *invite my friends over to watch the Super Bowl*

8. *have some "peace and quiet" around the house*

THEY WISH THEY LIVED IN THE CITY

The Anderson family lives in the suburbs, but they wish they lived in the city. If they lived in the city, Mr. Anderson wouldn't have to spend all his spare time mowing the lawn and working around the house. Mrs. Anderson wouldn't have to spend two hours commuting to work every day. Their son Michael would be able to take the bus to the baseball stadium. Their daughter, Jennifer, would be living close to all of her favorite book stores. And their other son, Steven, could visit the zoo more often. It would be very difficult for the Anderson family to move to the city now, but perhaps some day they'll be able to. They certainly hope so.

COMPLETE THE STORY

THEY WISH THEY LIVED IN THE SUBURBS

The Burton family lives in the city, but they _____ ¹ they lived in the suburbs. If they _____ ² in the suburbs, Mrs. Burton _____ ³ be able to plant a garden and grow vegetables. Mr. Burton _____ ⁴ have to listen to noisy city traffic all the time. Their son, Ken, _____ ⁵ have a backyard to play in. Their daughters, Betsy and Kathy, _____ ⁶ have to share a room. And their cat, Tiger, _____ ⁷ be able to go outside and play with the other cats. It _____ ⁸ be very difficult for the Burton family to move to the suburbs now, but perhaps some day they'll be _____ ⁹ to. They certainly hope so.

How About You?

Do you wish you lived someplace else? Where? Why?

Compare life in the city and life in the suburbs. What are the advantages and disadvantages of each?

READING

"ALL THUMBS"

Ethel can never fix anything around the house. In fact, everybody tells her she's "all thumbs." She wishes she were more mechanically inclined. If she were more mechanically inclined, she would be able to repair things around the house by herself.

Robert can't dance very well. In fact, all the girls he goes out with tell him he has "two left feet." Robert wishes he could dance better. If he could dance better, he wouldn't feel so self-conscious when he goes dancing.

Maria is having a hard time learning English. She's having a lot of trouble with English grammar and pronunciation. Maria wishes she had a "better ear" for languages. If she had a "better ear" for languages, she probably wouldn't be having so much trouble in her English class.

 READING *CHECK-UP*

MATCHING: *Do You Know These Expressions?*

____ **1.** He's *all thumbs*.

____ **2.** She's *handy* around the house.

____ **3.** He has *a green thumb*.

____ **4.** He's *all heart*.

____ **5.** He's very *nosey*.

____ **6.** She's got *a lot on her shoulders*.

____ **7.** She always *keeps her chin up*.

____ **8.** He's *up in arms*.

a. very kind

b. doesn't know how to fix things

c. optimistic

d. knows how to fix things

e. has many responsibilities

f. good at gardening

g. very angry

h. asks about other people

How About You?

Are you "all thumbs"? Do you have "two left feet"? Everybody has a few things he or she would like to do better. What do you wish you could do better? Why?

LISTENING

Listen and choose the statement that is true based on what you hear.

1. a. He has a dog.
   b. He doesn't have a dog.

2. a. She works the night shift.
   b. She works the day shift.

3. a. She's a musician.
   b. She's a teacher.

4. a. He doesn't have to take biology.
   b. He has to take biology.

5. a. She can't type fast.
   b. She can type fast.

6. a. They don't have a car.
   b. They don't live in the city.

PRONUNCIATION Reduced *would*

Listen. Then say it.

Do you think the boss would be angry?

Do you think the neighbors would be annoyed?

Do you think Roy would be jealous?

Do you think Ted would be disappointed?

Say it. Then listen.

Do you think my parents would be disappointed?

Do you think the voters would be upset?

Do you think Julie would be mad?

Do you think Matt would be embarrassed?

Write in your journal about something in your life you wish for. What do you wish? How would your life be different if your wish came true?

GRAMMAR FOCUS

PRESENT UNREAL CONDITIONAL (IF ___ WOULD)

Do you think the boss **would** be angry **if** I went home early?
I **wouldn't** go home early **if** I were you.

If	I he she we you they	could dance,	I'd he'd she'd we'd you'd they'd	go dancing.

If my TV weren't fixed,	**I could** **I'd be able to**	talk with my children.

WISH-CLAUSES

I We You They	wish	I we you they	lived in New York. were more athletic. could dance. didn't live here. weren't sick.
He She	wishes	he she	

Complete the sentences.

1. I don't enjoy working the night shift. I wish I _____ the day shift.

2. Gregory doesn't enjoy being a salesperson. He wishes he _____ the store manager.

3. If I _____ you, I _____ skip class tomorrow. I'm sure the teacher _____ _____ upset.

4. I wish I _____ fix my car by myself. If I _____ do that, _____ save a lot of money on repairs.

5. If I _____ you, I _____ order the spicy stew. If you _____ it, _____ probably get a bad stomachache.

6. We're busy tomorrow night. If we _____ busy, _____ be happy to see a movie with you.

7. I have a meeting this afternoon. If I _____ have a meeting, _____ be able to drive you to the airport.

8. I _____ buy a TV at Al's Discount Store if I _____ you. If you _____ a TV at Al's, _____ probably regret it.

Past Unreal Conditional
(If _____ Would Have)
Wish-Clauses (continued)

- Asking for and Giving Reasons
- Making Deductions
- Discussing Unexpected Events
- Expressing Wishes and Hopes
- Consequences of Actions
- Rumors

VOCABULARY PREVIEW

1. audience
2. cactus plant
3. chemistry set
4. flu shot
5. income tax form
6. ingredients
7. metal detector
8. minister
9. mortgage
10. performance
11. postcard
12. printer
13. snowman
14. traffic light
15. wedding dress

If She Had Known . . .

if _____ would have _____

| I |
| He |
| She |
| It | would have eaten. |
| We |
| You |
| They |

A. Why didn't Brenda take her umbrella to work today?

B. She didn't know it was going to rain.
If she had known it was going to rain, she would have taken her umbrella to work today.

A. Why weren't you in class yesterday?

B. I wasn't feeling well.
If I had been feeling well, I would have been in class yesterday.

1. Why didn't Jason stop at the traffic light?
He didn't notice it.
If _____.

2. Why didn't you go to the movies last night?
I wasn't in the mood to see a film.
If _____.

3. Why wasn't Mark on time for work today?
His alarm clock didn't ring.
If _____.

4. Why didn't you hand in your paper today?
My printer wasn't working last night.
If _____.

5. Why didn't the Kramers buy the house on Pine Street?
Their mortgage wasn't approved.
If _____.

6. Why didn't Mr. and Mrs. Park enjoy their ski vacation?
There wasn't enough snow.
If _____.

7. Why didn't you send us a postcard?
We didn't remember your address.
If _____.

8. Why didn't you go to the party last night?
I wasn't invited.
If _____.

9. Why didn't Mr. and Mrs. Sanchez enjoy the play last night?
They didn't have good seats.
If _____.

10. Why wasn't Senator Harrington re-elected?
The people didn't trust him.
If _____.

11. Why didn't Mr. Kelly's students give him a birthday present?
He didn't tell them it was his birthday.
If _____.

12. Why wasn't Sophia asked to sing an encore last night?
The audience wasn't pleased with her performance.
If _____.

I Wonder Why

A. I wonder why Charles ran by without saying hello.

B. He must have been in a hurry.

A. You're probably right. If he hadn't been in a hurry, he wouldn't have run by without saying hello.

1. I wonder why the boss was so irritable today.
be upset about something

2. I wonder why Pamela arrived late for work.
miss the bus

3. I wonder why Larry quit.
find a better job

4. I wonder why Donna went home early today.
be feeling "under the weather"

5. I wonder why Rover got sick last night.
eat something he shouldn't have

6. I wonder why Jill prepared so much food.
expect a lot of people to come to her party

7. I wonder why Diane went to sleep so early.
have a hard day at the office

8. I wonder why my shirt shrank* so much.
be 100 percent cotton

9. I wonder why my computer shut down.
run out of power

10. I wonder why my cactus plant died.
have a rare disease

11. I wonder why Mom got stopped by a police officer.
be driving too fast

12. I wonder why Dad got searched by the security person.
set off the metal detector

13. I wonder why the minister arrived late for the wedding.
get lost

14.

*shrink - shrank - shrunk

UNEXPECTED GUESTS

Melba had a very difficult situation at her house a few days ago. Her relatives from Minneapolis arrived unexpectedly, without any advance notice whatsoever, and they stayed for the entire weekend.

Needless to say, Melba was very upset. If she had known that her relatives from Minneapolis were going to arrive and stay for the entire weekend, she would have been prepared for their visit. She would have bought a lot of food. She would have cleaned the house. And she certainly wouldn't have invited all her daughter's friends from nursery school to come over and play.

Poor Melba! She really wishes her relatives had called in advance to say they were coming.

✔ READING CHECK-UP

TRUE, FALSE, OR MAYBE?

Answer True, False, or Maybe (if the answer isn't in the story).

1. Melba lives in Minneapolis.
2. Her relatives didn't call to say they were coming.
3. If Melba's relatives hadn't arrived unexpectedly, she would have been prepared for their visit.
4. When her relatives arrived, Melba was upset, but she didn't say so.
5. If her house had been clean and she had had more food, Melba would have been more prepared for her relatives' unexpected visit.
6. Melba's relatives realized they should have called in advance to say they were coming.

WHAT'S THE WORD?

Complete these sentences using *would have* or *wouldn't have* and the correct form of the verb.

1. If the plane had arrived on time, I (*be*) _____ late for the meeting.
2. If the weather had been nice yesterday, we (*go*) _____ to the beach.
3. If I hadn't been out of town, I (*miss*) _____ my daughter's soccer game.
4. If I had seen that stop sign, Officer, I certainly (*drive*) _____ through it.
5. If the president hadn't been in a hurry, he (*give*) _____ a longer speech.
6. If I had known you were a vegetarian, I (*make*) _____ beef stew.

How About You?

Have you ever had a difficult situation when something unexpected happened and you weren't prepared? Tell about it.

WISHING IT HAD HAPPENED DIFFERENTLY

Andrew didn't save his work on his computer yesterday. He really wishes he had saved it. If he had saved it, he wouldn't have lost his history paper. And if he hadn't lost his history paper, he would have been able to hand it in on time today.

Marilyn's alarm clock didn't ring this morning. She really wishes it had rung. If it had rung, she wouldn't have been late for work this morning. And if she hadn't been late, her supervisor wouldn't have scolded her.

Stan filled out his income tax form very quickly this year. He really wishes he had filled it out more carefully. If he had filled it out more carefully, he wouldn't have made so many mistakes. And if he hadn't made so many mistakes, he wouldn't have gotten into trouble with the Internal Revenue Service.

Mr. and Mrs. Carson didn't follow the directions on the box when they baked cookies yesterday. They really wish they had. If they had followed the directions, they would have used the right ingredients. And if they had used the right ingredients, the cookies wouldn't have been as hard as rocks!

READING CHECK-UP

TRUE, FALSE, OR MAYBE?

Answer True, False, or Maybe (if the answer isn't in the story).

1. Andrew handed in his history paper on time.
2. He wishes he had saved his work on his computer.
3. Marilyn's supervisor didn't scold her.
4. If Stan hadn't completed the form quickly, he wouldn't have made any mistakes.
5. Mr. and Mrs. Carson's cookies would have been softer if they hadn't used the wrong ingredients.

How About You?

Have you ever done something and then regretted it? Tell about something you wish you had done differently, and why.

I Wish

| I **live** in Boston. | I **lived** in Boston. |
| I **wish** I **lived** in New York. | I **wish** I **had lived** in New York. |

A. I wish I knew my neighbors.

B. Why do you say that?

A. If I knew my neighbors, I wouldn't be so lonely.

B. I know what you mean.

A. I wish I had known how to get around town when I moved here.

B. Why do you say that?

A. If I had known how to get around town when I moved here, I wouldn't have been so confused.

B. I know what you mean.

1. I don't drive to work. ☹
I have to wait for the train every morning.

2. I didn't drive to work today. ☹
I had to wait an hour for the bus.

102

3. I don't do daily exercises. ☹
   I have to go on a diet.

4. I didn't do my homework last night. ☹
   I had to do it early this morning.

5. I don't have a good job. ☹
   I'm concerned about my future.

6. I didn't have a flu shot last fall. ☹
   I was sick all winter.

7. I'm not an optimist. ☹
   I get depressed so often.

8. I wasn't prepared for my math test. ☹
   I got a low grade.

9. My husband and I don't take dance
   lessons. ☹
   We feel "out of place" at parties.

10. I didn't take medicine when my tooth
    began to hurt. ☹
    I felt miserable all day.

How to Say It!

Empathizing

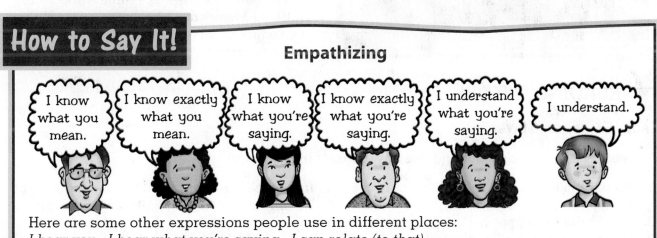

I know what you mean.

I know exactly what you mean.

I know what you're saying.

I know exactly what you're saying.

I understand what you're saying.

I understand.

Here are some other expressions people use in different places:
I hear you. I hear what you're saying. I can relate (to that).

Practice the conversations in this lesson again. Use different expressions for empathizing.

RUMORS

All the people at the office are talking about Samantha these days. There's a rumor that Samantha is going to be transferred to the company's office in Paris, and everybody is convinced that the rumor is true. After all, if she weren't going to be transferred to the company's office in Paris, she wouldn't have put her condo up for sale. She wouldn't have started taking French lessons. And she DEFINITELY wouldn't have broken up with her boyfriend.

Of course, the people at the office don't know for sure whether Samantha is going to be transferred to the company's office in Paris. It's only a rumor. They'll just have to wait and see.

All the assembly-line workers at the National Motors automobile company are worrying about the future these days. There's a rumor that the factory is going to close down soon, and everybody is convinced that the rumor is true. After all, if the factory weren't going to close down soon, everybody on the night shift wouldn't have been laid off. The managers wouldn't all be reading the want ads and working on their resumes. And the boss DEFINITELY wouldn't have canceled the annual company picnic!

Of course, the assembly-line workers at National Motors don't know for sure whether the factory is going to close down soon. It's only a rumor. They'll just have to wait and see.

✔ READING *CHECK-UP*

TRUE, FALSE, OR MAYBE?

Answer True, False, or Maybe (if the answer isn't in the story).

1. Samantha is going to be transferred to the company's office in Paris.
2. Samantha hasn't put her condo up for sale.
3. The people at the office think Samantha wouldn't have broken up with her boyfriend if she weren't going to be transferred.
4. There's a rumor that workers on the night shift at the National Motors factory are going to lose their jobs.
5. There isn't going to be a company picnic this year.
6. The factory is going to close down soon.

CHOOSE

1. The students in our class were upset when our teacher quit last week.
   a. We won't be upset if she doesn't quit.
   b. We wouldn't be upset if she didn't quit.
   c. We wouldn't have been upset if she hadn't quit.

2. I didn't come over to your table and have lunch with you because I didn't see you in the cafeteria.
   a. If I saw you, I would have come over and had lunch with you.
   b. If I had seen you, I would have come over and had lunch with you.
   c. If I had seen you, I would come over and have lunch with you.

3. I'm afraid I can't help you type those letters because I'm going to leave work early today.
   a. If I weren't going to leave work early, I'd help you type those letters.
   b. If I were going to leave work early, I'd help you type those letters.
   c. If I were going to leave work early, I wouldn't help you type those letters.

4. Betsy didn't take her umbrella to work today. She got wet on the way home.
   a. If she hadn't taken her umbrella to work, she wouldn't have gotten wet.
   b. If she had taken her umbrella to work, she wouldn't have gotten wet.
   c. If she hadn't taken her umbrella to work, she would have gotten wet.

LISTENING

Listen and choose the statement that is true based on what you hear.

1. a. She's rich.
   b. She isn't rich.

2. a. He remembered her e-mail address.
   b. He didn't remember her e-mail address.

3. a. They would have enjoyed the game more if they had had better seats.
   b. They wouldn't have enjoyed the game more if they had had better seats.

4. a. The boys in the hallway aren't the landlord's children.
   b. The boys in the hallway are the landlord's children.

5. a. He wasn't hired for the job.
   b. He was hired for the job.

6. a. Johnny's grandparents are at his party.
   b. Johnny's grandparents couldn't come to his party.

IN YOUR OWN WORDS

FOR WRITING AND DISCUSSION

Have you heard any rumors lately at school or at work? Tell a story about a rumor.

What's the rumor?
Do you think the rumor is true?
Why or why not?

ON YOUR OWN *Wishes and Hopes*

> I hope it's sunny tomorrow.   (It might be sunny.)
> I wish it were sunny.   (It isn't sunny.)
> I wish it had been sunny   (It wasn't sunny.)
>   during our picnic.

Practice these conversations.

1.

> A. I hope it's a nice day tomorrow.
>
> B. Why?
>
> A. If it's a nice day tomorrow, we'll be able to go to the beach.

2.

> A. I wish I were taller.
>
> B. How come?
>
> A. If I were taller, I'd be able to play on the basketball team.

3.

> A. I wish I had saved my wedding dress.
>
> B. Why do you say that?
>
> A. If I had saved my wedding dress, you could have worn it today at your wedding.

What do you hope? What do you wish? Share your thoughts with other students.

PRONUNCIATION   Reduced *have*

Listen. Then say it.

They would have enjoyed their vacation.

He wouldn't have arrived late.

She would have taken her umbrella.

I wouldn't have quit.

Say it. Then listen.

We would have used the right ingredients.

They wouldn't have invited so many people.

He would have been on time.

It wouldn't have shrunk.

 Write in your journal about something in your life that you wish you had done, but didn't. What do you wish you had done? Why? What would have happened in your life if you had done that?

GRAMMAR FOCUS

PAST UNREAL CONDITIONAL (IF ___ WOULD HAVE)

If	I he she we you they	had known,	I he she we you they	**would have** told them.

If	I he she we you they	hadn't missed the bus,	I he she we you they	**wouldn't have** been late.

WISH-CLAUSES

I We You They	wish	I we you they	had gone there. hadn't gone there.
He She	wishes	he she	

I live in New York.
I wish I lived in California.

I don't know my neighbors.
I wish I knew my neighbors.

I lived in Boston.
I wish I had lived in Miami.

I didn't do that.
I wish I had done that.

Choose the correct word.

1. Rita worked twelve hours yesterday and fell asleep at 9 P.M. If she (hadn't worked   didn't work) so many hours, she probably (wouldn't fall   wouldn't have fallen) asleep so early.

2. I didn't enjoy the play because I didn't have a good seat. If I (had   had had) a good seat, I (would have enjoyed   would enjoy) the play.

3. Susan didn't come to my party last Friday because she had to work overtime. If she (hasn't had   hadn't had) to work overtime, she (would have come   would come) to my party.

4. I arrived late for the meeting because I got lost. If I (didn't get   hadn't gotten) lost, I (didn't arrive   wouldn't have arrived) late.

5. George is lonely because he doesn't know his neighbors. He wishes he (had known   knew) them. If he (didn't know   knew) them, he (wouldn't be   wouldn't have been) so lonely.

6. I got a low grade on my history exam because I wasn't prepared for it. I really wish I (was   had been) prepared for it. If I (had been   weren't) prepared for the exam, I (wouldn't get   wouldn't have gotten) a low grade.

Reported Speech
Sequence of Tenses

VOCABULARY PREVIEW

1. bride	6. college entrance exam	11. navy
2. groom	7. dictionary	12. pipe
3. interviewer	8. engine	13. puppy
4. movie star	9. lion	14. radiator
5. school-bus driver	10. message	15. robbery

What Did She Say?

"**I'm** busy."		he **was** busy.
"**I'm working** hard."		he **was working** hard.
"**I like** jazz."		he **liked** jazz.
"**I'm going to** buy a new car."		he **was going to** buy a new car.
"**I went** to Paris last year."	He said (that)*	he **had gone** to Paris last year.
"**I was** in London last week."		he **had been** in London last week.
"**I've seen** the movie."		he **had seen** the movie.
"**I'll call** the doctor."		he **would call** the doctor.
"**I can** help you."		he **could** help me.

I'm sick.

A. I forgot to tell you. Grandma called yesterday.

B. Really? What did she say?

A. She said (that)* **she was sick**.

A. I forgot to tell you. _____ called yesterday.

B. Really? What did _____ say?

A. _____ said (that)* _____.

We're engaged.

1. *Miguel and Maria*

I'm doing very well in college this semester.

2. *Robert*

* Or: "He / She / They told me (that)"

3. *Aunt Margaret*

4. *our upstairs neighbors*

5. *our niece Terry*

6. *Uncle Ted*

7. *your brother in Detroit*

8. *your sister in Seattle*

9. *the woman from the furniture store*

10. *the TV repairman*

11. *my boss*

12. *our nephew Paul*

13. *the little girl down the street*

14. *the auto mechanic*

15. *my boyfriend*

16. *Uncle Frank*

111

Haven't You Heard?

John **is** sick.

I knew
I didn't know } (that) John **was** sick.

A. What's everybody talking about?

B. Haven't you heard? Our English teacher is in the hospital!

A. You're kidding! I didn't know (that) our English teacher was in the hospital.

B. You didn't?! I thought EVERYBODY knew (that) our English teacher was in the hospital!

A. What's everybody _____ about?

B. Haven't you heard? _____!

A. You're kidding! I didn't know (that) _____.

B. You didn't?! I thought EVERYBODY knew (that) _____!

Jack is going to be a father!

1. What's everybody talking about?

Our landlord wants to sell the building!

2. What's everybody so upset about?

3. What's everybody so happy about?

4. What's everybody so nervous about?

5. What's everybody so angry about?

6. What's everybody so happy about?

7. What's everybody so anxious about?

8. What's everybody so excited about?

9. What's everybody talking about?

10.

How to Say It!

Expressing Surprise

Practice the conversations in this lesson again. Express surprise in different ways.

READING

A LOT OF MESSAGES

Sally was home alone this afternoon while her parents were at work. There were a lot of phone calls, and Sally wrote down a lot of messages.

✓ READING CHECK-UP

Q & A

The next day, Sally was home alone again. Her mother called from the office. Create dialogs based on the following model and information.

1. Grandma • "Grandpa isn't feeling very well and wants me to call the doctor."
2. The landlord • "I received your check this morning."
3. Uncle Harry • "I'm getting married next month, and I want all of you to come to my wedding."

> A. Tell me, have there been any calls?
> B. Yes. _____ called.
> A. Oh? What did __ say?
> B. __ said _____.

4. The neighbors across the street • "The police caught the man who robbed our house."
5. The plumber • "I'm still sick, and I can't get there today."
6. Joe's Auto Repair Shop • "We've finished working on the engine, and the car is ready to be picked up."

COMPLETE THE STORY

Well, . . .

Your brother got engaged.

Your sister and brother-in-law are going to have a baby.

Your father is planning to retire next month.

There was a big fire at the high school.

The dog had six puppies.

And your high school sweetheart married a movie star and moved to Hollywood.

Aside from that, not much else happened.

Hi, Mom! What's new?

HOME FROM THE NAVY

Bill serves as a lieutenant in the navy. He returned home last weekend after being at sea for several months. Since he hadn't been in touch with his family for a long time, he was very surprised at all the things that had happened while he was away.

He didn't know his brother __had gotten__ [1] engaged. He also didn't know his sister and brother-in-law _____ [2] have a baby. And he was unaware that his father _____ [3] retire next month.

In addition, he didn't know there _____ [4] a big fire at the high school. He hadn't heard that the dog _____ [5] six puppies. And he had no idea that his high school sweetheart _____ [6] a movie star and _____ [7] to Hollywood.

A lot of things certainly had changed while Bill was away.

TRUE, FALSE, OR MAYBE?

Answer True, False, or Maybe (if the answer isn't in the story).

1. Bill has been on a ship for the past several months.
2. His sister had a baby while he was away.
3. His father has retired.

4. Bill's high school was very large.
5. Bill's former girlfriend lives in Hollywood now.

LISTENING

Listen and choose the statement that is true based on what you hear.

1. a. It snowed.
   b. It's still snowing.

2. a. He didn't know that his supervisor had been in the hospital.
   b. He didn't know that his supervisor was in the hospital.

3. a. She wasn't aware that jackets were on sale.
   b. She wasn't aware that jackets had been on sale.

4. a. He didn't know she had to work on Saturday.
   b. He didn't know she had worked on Saturday.

5. a. She was aware that Sherman had been thinking of leaving.
   b. She was unaware that Sherman had been thinking of leaving.

6. a. Her friends hadn't told her they were going to move.
   b. Her friends had told her they were going to move.

What Did They Ask?

"Where is the bank?"		where the bank was.
"When are you going to visit me?"		when I was going to visit him.
"Do you speak English?"	He asked me	$\left\{\begin{array}{l}\text{if}\\\text{whether}\end{array}\right\}$ I spoke English.
"Have you seen Mary?"		$\left\{\begin{array}{l}\text{if}\\\text{whether}\end{array}\right\}$ I had seen Mary.

A. You won't believe what a three-year-old boy asked me today!

B. What did he ask you?

A. He asked me why there was a Santa Claus in every department store in town.

B. I can't believe he asked you that!

A. I can't either.

A. You won't believe what my boss asked me today!

B. What did she ask you?

A. She asked me $\left\{\begin{array}{l}\text{if}\\\text{whether}\end{array}\right\}$ I wanted to receive a raise this year.

B. I can't believe she asked you that!

A. I can't either.

A. You won't believe what _____ asked me today!

B. What did _____ ask you?

A. _____ asked me _____.

B. I can't believe _____ asked you that!

A. I can't either.

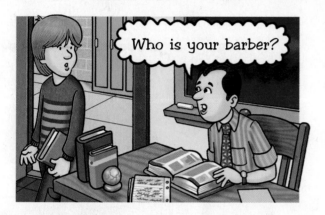

1. *my history teacher*

2. *my boyfriend*

3. *my nine-year-old nephew*

4. *the woman at my job interview*

5. *my students*

6. *my parents*

(continued)

7. *my philosophy professor*

8. *my daughter*

9. *my basketball coach*

10. *my son*

11. *a taxi driver*

12. *the patient in Room 12*

13. *Grandma*

14.

Where did you go to school?

Have you had any special training?

Where have you worked?

Are you willing to move to another city?

Can you work overtime and weekends?

How is your health?

Have you ever been fired?

Why did you have four different jobs last year?

Why do you think you're more qualified for the position than the other sixty-two people who have applied?

THE JOB INTERVIEW

Charles had a job interview a few days ago at the United Insurance Company. The interview lasted almost an hour, and Charles had to answer a lot of questions.

First, the interviewer asked Charles where he had gone to school. Then she asked if he had had any special training. She asked where he had worked. She also asked whether he was willing to move to another city. She wanted to know if he could work overtime and weekends. She asked him how his health was. She asked him whether he had ever been fired. She wanted to know why he had had four different jobs last year.

And finally, the interviewer asked the most difficult question. She wanted to know why Charles thought he was more qualified for the position than the other sixty-two people who had applied.

Charles had never been asked so many questions at a job interview before. He doesn't know how well he did, but he tried his best.

 ## READING *CHECK-UP*

ROLE PLAY

You're applying for a job at the United Insurance Company. Role-play a job interview with another student, using the questions in the illustration as a guide.

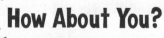

Tell about a job interview you had.
   Where was the interview?
   How long did it last?
   What questions did the interviewer ask?
   What were your answers?
   What was the most difficult question, and how did you answer it?
   Did you get the job?

Job interviewers sometimes like to ask difficult questions. Why do you think they do this? What are some difficult questions interviewers might ask? Make a list, and think of answers to those questions.

What Did They Tell You?

"Call me after five o'clock."	to call him after five o'clock.
"Stop complaining!"	to stop complaining.
	He told me
"Don't worry!"	not to worry.
"Don't call me before nine o'clock."	not to call him before nine o'clock.

Keep your dog in the house! I'm afraid to deliver your mail!

A. I'm a little annoyed at the mailman.

B. How come?

A. He told me to keep my dog in the house.

B. Why did he tell you that?

A. He said (that) he was afraid to deliver my mail.

Don't play your music so loud! You're bothering us!

A. I'm a little annoyed at my neighbors.

B. How come?

A. They told me not to play my music so loud.

B. Why did they tell you that?

A. They said (that) I was bothering them.

A. I'm a little annoyed at _____.
B. How come?
A. ____ told me _____.
B. Why did ____ tell you that?
A. ____ said (that) _____.

1. *my doctor*

2. *my dentist*

3. *my math teacher*

4. *the school-bus driver*

5. *my girlfriend*

6. *my parents*

7. *my boss*

8. *my landlord*

9. *my seven-year-old son*

How About You?

Do you remember the last time someone said something that really annoyed you?
What did the person say? (*He/She told me . . .*)
Why do you think he/she said that?
Did you say anything back?

READING

GOOD ADVICE

Margaret had a bad stomachache yesterday afternoon. She called her doctor and asked him what she should do. Her doctor told her to rest in bed. He also told her not to eat too much for dinner. And he told her to call him in the morning if she was still sick. Margaret felt better after speaking with her doctor. She's glad she can always depend on him for good advice.

Eric went out on his first date yesterday evening. Before he left the house, he asked his parents if they had any advice. They told him to be polite when he met the girl's mother and father. They also told him not to drive too fast. And they told him not to bring his date home later than ten o'clock. Eric felt more prepared for his date after speaking to his parents. He's glad he can always depend on them for good advice.

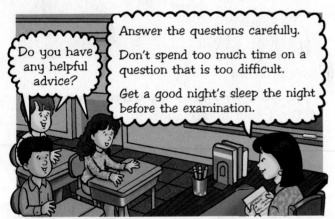

Mrs. Tanaka's students are going to take the college entrance examination this Saturday, and they're very nervous. They asked Mrs. Tanaka if she had any helpful advice. She told them to answer the questions carefully. She also told them not to spend too much time on a question that was too difficult. And she told them to get a good night's sleep the night before the examination. Mrs. Tanaka's students felt more confident after speaking with her. They're glad they can always depend on her for good advice.

Mr. and Mrs. Pratt are going away on vacation soon, and they're concerned because there have been several robberies in their neighborhood recently. They called the police and asked them what they could do to prevent their house from being broken into while they were away. The police told them to lock all the windows and leave on a few lights. They also advised them to ask the neighbors to pick up the mail. And they warned them not to tell too many people that they would be away. Mr. and Mrs. Pratt felt reassured after speaking with the police. They're glad they can always depend on them for good advice.

✔ READING *CHECK-UP*

TRUE, FALSE, OR MAYBE?

Answer True, False, or Maybe (if the answer isn't in the story).

1. Margaret told her doctor to rest in bed.
2. Margaret didn't eat very much for dinner yesterday.
3. Eric hadn't gone out on a date before yesterday.
4. Eric brought his date home by ten o'clock.
5. Mrs. Tanaka teaches at a college.
6. Mrs. Tanaka got a good night's sleep the night before the examination.
7. Locking windows and leaving on lights are two ways to prevent robberies.
8. The Pratts' house was broken into while they were away.

CHOOSE

1. Eric's parents told him _____.
   a. not to drive too fast
   b. don't drive too fast

2. Mrs. Tanaka told her students _____.
   a. answer the questions carefully
   b. to answer the questions carefully

3. She told him _____.
   a. don't worry
   b. not to worry

4. She asked _____ a vegetarian.
   a. if I was
   b. whether are you

5. My friends said that _____.
   a. they will be here
   b. they would be here

6. We _____ them to call us.
   a. said
   b. told

PRONUNCIATION   Reduced *to*

Listen. Then say it.

He told me to sit down.

She told me not to call her.

She asked me where I went to school.

They said they wouldn't be able to come to the party.

Say it. Then listen.

She told me to lose some weight.

He told me not to eat candy.

He asked me if I wanted to get married.

She said I didn't have to work overtime.

Write in your journal about a time when you needed advice. Why did you need advice? (What was the situation?) Who did you ask for advice? What did you ask? What did the person tell you? Did you follow the person's advice? Was it good advice or bad advice? Why?

GRAMMAR FOCUS

"I'm busy."		he was busy.
"I like jazz."		he liked jazz.
"I'm going to buy a new car."		he was going to buy a new car.
"I went to Paris last year."	He said (that)	he had gone to Paris last year.
"I was in London last week."		he had been in London last week.
"I've seen the movie."		he had seen the movie.
"I'll call the doctor."		he would call the doctor.
"I can help you."		he could help me.

John is sick.			John was sick.
Jack is going to be a father.	I knew (that)		Jack was going to be a father.
Our landlord wants to sell the building.	I didn't know (that)		our landlord wanted to sell the building.
We can't use our dictionaries.			we couldn't use our dictionaries.

"Where is the bank?"		where the bank was.
"When are you going to visit me?"		when I was going to visit him.
"Do you speak English?"	He asked me	{ if / whether } I spoke English.
"Have you seen Mary?"		{ if / whether } I had seen Mary.

"Call me after five o'clock."		to call him after five o'clock.
"Stop complaining!"		to stop complaining.
"Don't worry!"	He told me	not to worry.
"Don't call me before nine o'clock."		not to call him before nine o'clock.

Choose the correct word.

1. Jessica called. She told me (if she likes   she liked) her new job very much.

2. Richard said (he was   if he's) sorry he (wouldn't   won't) be able to help us move.

3. Did Uncle Walter (tell   ask) you (did he get   he had gotten) fired from his job?

4. Ms. Chen called. She told me (she couldn't   if she can) come to the meeting tomorrow.

5. I didn't know (we didn't   don't we) have to come to work early tomorrow morning.

6. I just spoke to Marta. She told me (has she been   she had been) promoted again.

7. My secretary said he (was   is) sorry he (hasn't   hadn't) finished the report on time.

8. My parents asked me (when are my exams   when my exams were).

9. The interviewer asked me where (I had gone   did I go) to school.

10. My doctor is concerned. She told me (to lose   must I lose) fifteen pounds.

11. Our landlord told us (to don't play   not to play) loud music after midnight.

12. The waiter (asked   told) me (do I want   if I wanted) to order dessert.

13. The nurse (told   asked) me (if I had ever   have I ever) had a flu shot.

Feature Article		Global Exchange
Fact File	SIDE *by* SIDE **Gazette**	Listening
Around the World		Fun with Idioms
Interview		What Are They
We've Got Mail!		Saying?

Volume 4   Number 3

Polish Up Your Interview Skills!

Tips from the experts

Going to a job interview can be a very challenging experience. A lot of people are probably applying for the same job. What can you do to make a good impression and stand out from the crowd?

The experts say, "Be prepared!" Learn about the company before your interview. Find out about the company's products or services. Read about the company in the newspaper, or try to find information on the Internet. (Many companies have their own websites with lots of information.) Also, dress appropriately for the interview. Don't wear casual clothes. Dress neatly and conservatively.

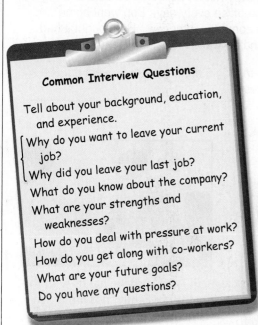

Common Interview Questions

Tell about your background, education, and experience.

Why do you want to leave your current job?

Why did you leave your last job?

What do you know about the company?

What are your strengths and weaknesses?

How do you deal with pressure at work?

How do you get along with co-workers?

What are your future goals?

Do you have any questions?

Prepare in advance for the types of questions you will probably be asked. The interviewer will most likely ask you to tell about your background, education, and experience. If you are employed, the interviewer may ask you why you want to leave your current job. Or, if you aren't employed at the time of the interview, the interviewer might ask why you left your last job. You should be prepared to talk about what you know about the company. Don't be surprised if you are asked what your strengths and weaknesses are. Be ready to answer questions about how you deal with pressure at work. An interviewer will most likely ask you how you get along with co-workers. You may also be asked what your future goals are. And don't forget that the interviewer will probably ask if you have any questions.

Be sure to answer the interviewer's questions honestly. Try to show that you are motivated, responsible, and very interested in the job. Be confident, but don't brag about yourself. (Don't say how great you are. Instead, give examples of things you've done that show your strengths.)

Be prepared for when the interviewer asks if you have any questions. You can ask about the job responsibilities, the company in general, when the position will be filled, and other things. Some experts say that it isn't a good idea to ask too many questions about salary, vacations, or benefits during the first interview. If the company has follow-up interviews for the position, that might be a better time for such questions. Before you leave the interview, make sure you know the names and titles of all the people you met. Write a thank-you letter to the interviewer as soon as possible. Say thank you for the interviewer's time, describe why you think you're the right person for the job, and offer to go back for another interview if they want you to.

FACT FILE

How People Find Jobs

want ads 14%
networking 35%
employment agencies 11%
other 10%
contacting employer directly 30%

Who Got the Job?

Sarah Jones went to a job interview yesterday at a computer software company. First, the interviewer asked her about her background and experience. She told about where she had gone to school, what she had studied, and what kinds of jobs she had had. When the interviewer asked

her why she wanted to leave her current job, she said that she was looking for a more challenging position. Then the interviewer asked Sarah what she knew about the company. She answered that she used some of the company's software and she had read articles about the company in the newspaper. Then the interviewer asked what her strengths and weaknesses were. She replied that she worked very hard and got along well with people, but she had some problems writing business letters. She explained that she was now taking a business writing class at a local college. Finally, the interviewer asked Sarah if she had any questions. Sarah asked if the job required a lot of travel, and she asked what the company's plans for the future were. As soon as she got home, Sarah wrote a thank-you note to the interviewer.

Bob Mills went to a job interview yesterday at the same company. First, the interviewer asked him about his background and experience. Bob said he had listed all that information on his resume and the interviewer could find it there. When the interviewer

asked him why he wanted to change employers, Bob replied that he was looking for a job with shorter hours and fewer responsibilities. Then the interviewer asked what he knew about the company. Bob said he wasn't really familiar with the company's products, and he asked what they were. When the interviewer asked what his strengths and weaknesses were, Bob said he hadn't really thought about that before, but it was a good question. Finally, the interviewer asked Bob if he had any questions. Bob asked if he could have 25 vacation days during his first year, and he wanted to know whether he would be able to bring his dog to the office every day. Bob went home feeling good about the interview. He thought it had gone well, and he waited for the company to call.

Who do you think got the job? For fun, act out the two interviews!

AROUND THE WORLD

Job Interviews

Job interviews can be very different around the world. An interviewer's questions, the "body language" that should be used, and the formality of an interview vary from country to country.

If you're at a job interview in Japan, don't look directly into the eyes of the interviewer. It is considered rude. But if you're at an interview in the United States, you should definitely make eye contact with the interviewer. If you don't, the interviewer may think you aren't trustworthy or confident.

In the United States and some other countries, interviewers aren't supposed to ask questions about family, marital status, and other personal information. In most countries, however, personal questions are very common during job interviews.

In France, shake hands with the interviewer lightly, not firmly. In many other countries, you should shake hands firmly, because a firm handshake is a sign of confidence. In Germany, your interview might begin with a very short informal conversation followed by a formal interview. In Mexico and many other countries, the informal small talk might take longer, and in some cases the entire interview might be informal.

What are job interviews like in countries you know?

Interview

A Side by Side Gazette reporter recently interviewed Monica Salinas, a Human Resources manager for a large insurance company. As a job interviewer, Ms. Salinas reads thousands of resumes and interviews hundreds of people each year.

Q: Tell us about your job.

A: I'm responsible for interviewing applicants for all the available positions in our company. Our firm is very large, so we receive more than 50 resumes and interview up to ten people each day. It's a lot of work!

Q: What are your favorite interview questions?

A: I like to ask applicants how they think other people would describe them. I also like to ask about weekend activities, hobbies, and other things that help me get to know the applicant as a person.

Q: What was your most memorable interview?

A: It was with a young woman from Brazil. She had only been in this country for four years. When she arrived, she didn't speak a word of English. But at her interview, her English was excellent! She said she had taken English courses and then studied business at a community college. She said she was the first person from her family to go to college. She impressed me so much. I asked her how she could contribute to our company. She said she would be the hardest worker here. Well, she is! I hired her, and last month she was chosen "Employee of the Year" and received a big bonus check. I asked her what she was going to do with the extra money. She said that she had already sent it to her family in Brazil so they could start building a new home.

Q: Have you had any unusual interviews?

A: One applicant said he was hungry. He opened a paper bag, took out a sandwich, and ate during the entire interview! Another time, an applicant was so nervous that she fainted. I got her some water, and I offered to reschedule the interview. She was lying on the floor, but she said that she was okay and wanted to continue. So I sat with her on the floor, and we had a very nice conversation.

Q: What is your best piece of advice for someone going to a job interview?

A: Be yourself! Smile, relax, and be honest. Let the interviewer see who you really are.

FUN with IDIOMS

Do You Know These Expressions?

____ 1. Don't put your foot in your mouth!

____ 2. Don't talk the interviewer's head off!

____ 3. Don't inflate your resume!

____ 4. Don't beat around the bush!

a. Answer questions briefly!

b. Answer questions directly!

c. Don't say the wrong thing!

d. Don't exaggerate your skills or experience!

We've Got Mail!

Dear Side by Side,

I have a question about tenses and reported speech. I understand that this is the correct way to say each of these sentences:

He said (that) he **was** hungry.

She told me (that) she **was** sick.

They said (that) they **were** engaged.

However, I often hear English speakers say:

He said (that) he **is** hungry.

She told me (that) she **is** sick.

They said (that) they **are** engaged.

Are both ways correct? I'm very confused.

Sincerely,

"Tense About Reported Speech"

Dear "Tense About Reported Speech,"

The first way to say these sentences is grammatically correct. However, in informal speech, the second way is also correct, especially when the person is reporting about something that someone has just said. We also "break the rule" when we talk about facts that are always true. For example:

We knew (that) Paris **is** the capital of France.

The teacher said (that) the Amazon **is** the longest river.

We hope this answers your question. Thanks for writing.

Sincerely,

Side by Side

Global Exchange

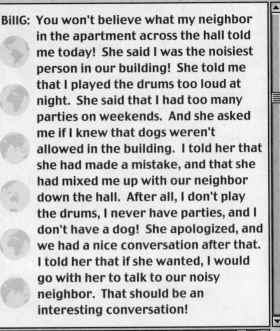

BillG: You won't believe what my neighbor in the apartment across the hall told me today! She said I was the noisiest person in our building! She told me that I played the drums too loud at night. She said that I had too many parties on weekends. And she asked me if I knew that dogs weren't allowed in the building. I told her that she had made a mistake, and that she had mixed me up with our neighbor down the hall. After all, I don't play the drums, I never have parties, and I don't have a dog! She apologized, and we had a nice conversation after that. I told her that if she wanted, I would go with her to talk to our noisy neighbor. That should be an interesting conversation!

Send a message to a keypal. Tell about an interesting conversation you have had.

What Are They Saying?

LISTENING

You Have Six Messages!

1. **a.** Jim Gavin wanted to know why money had been taken out of his paycheck.
   b. Jim Gavin wanted to know why money hadn't been taken out of his paycheck.

2. **a.** Denise said she hadn't been able to go to the meeting.
   b. Denise said she wouldn't be able to go to the meeting.

3. **a.** Patty told Joe that she had ordered more pens.
   b. Patty told Joe that she had canceled the order for pens.

4. **a.** Jane Adams called to say that the painters hadn't arrived yet.
   b. Jane Adams called to tell Joe when the painters would arrive.

5. **a.** George asked Joe if he could go to a doctor's appointment tomorrow morning.
   b. George told Joe that he would be at a doctor's appointment tomorrow morning.

6. **a.** Michelle told Joe she had taken a job with another company.
   b. Michelle told Joe that another company had offered her a job.

9

Tag Questions
Emphatic Sentences

- Verifying
- Expressing Surprise
- Reporting Information
- Congratulating
- Initiating Topics

- Expressing Opinions
- Expressing Agreement
- Writing a Personal Letter
- Writing a Business Memo
- Performance on the Job

VOCABULARY PREVIEW

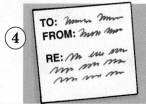

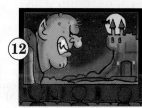

1. couple
2. dolphin
3. kite
4. memo

5. moon
6. spare tire
7. toaster
8. wagon

9. engaged
10. overcooked
11. punctual
12. scary

129

This Is the Bus to the Zoo, Isn't It?

Ken **is** here, **isn't** he? You **were** sick, **weren't** you? Maria **will** be here soon, **won't** she? Timmy **has** gone to bed, **hasn't** he? I **am** on time, **aren't** I?	You like ice cream, **don't** you? Ed worked yesterday, **didn't** he?

A. This is the bus to the zoo, isn't it?

B. Yes, it is.

A. That's what I thought.

1. Neil Armstrong was the first person on the moon, _____?

2. I can skateboard here, _____?

3. Ms. Lee will be on vacation next week, _____?

4. It's going to rain today, _____?

5. We've already seen this movie, _____?

6. I'm on time for my interview, _____?

7. You work in the Shipping Department, _____?

8. You locked the front door, _____?

9. You're a famous movie star, _____?

This TV Isn't On Sale This Week, Is It?

Bill **isn't** here, **is** he?
You **weren't** angry, **were** you?
Nina **won't** be upset, **will** she?
You **haven't** eaten, **have** you?
I**'m not** late, **am** I?

Mark **doesn't** ski, **does** he?
They **didn't** leave, **did** they?

A. This TV isn't on sale this week, is it?

B. No, it isn't.

A. That's what I thought.

1. There weren't any computers when you were young, _____?

2. I can't fish here, _____?

3. Mr. Martinez won't be in the office tomorrow, _____?

4. You aren't really going to go swimming, _____?

5. The mail hasn't come yet, _____?

6. I'm not allowed to park here, _____?

7. The children don't use this old wagon anymore, _____?

8. We didn't have a homework assignment yesterday, _____?

9. I haven't taught "tag questions" before, _____?

I'm Really Surprised!

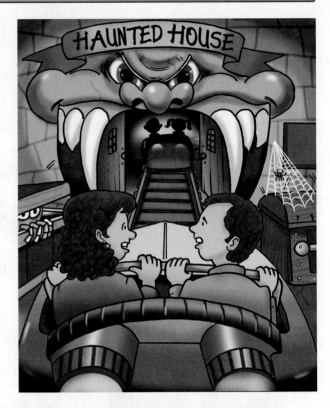

A. You like spaghetti, don't you?

B. Actually, I don't.

A. You DON'T?! I'm really surprised! I was SURE you liked spaghetti!

A. This ride isn't scary, is it?

B. Actually, it is.

A. It IS?! I'm really surprised! I was SURE this ride wasn't scary!

1. It's going to be a nice day tomorrow, _____?

2. I don't have to wear a jacket and tie here, _____?

3. This building has an elevator, _____?

4. You can swim, _____?

5. The bank hasn't closed yet, _____?

6. I did well on the exam, _____?

7. I'm going to play today, _____?

8. Dolphins can't talk, _____?

9. I wasn't going over fifty-five miles per hour, _____?

10. We have a spare tire, _____?

11. You aren't allergic to fish, _____?

12. I'm not a suspect, _____?

How to Say It!

Expressing Surprise

I'm really surprised!

I'm very surprised!

That's very surprising!

I can't believe it!

I don't believe it!

Practice the conversations in this lesson again. Express surprise in different ways.

Congratulations!

A. I have some good news.

B. What is it?

A. My wife and I are celebrating our fiftieth wedding anniversary tomorrow!

B. You ARE?!

A. Yes, we are.

B. I don't believe it! You aren't REALLY celebrating your fiftieth wedding anniversary tomorrow, are you?

A. Yes, it's true. We ARE.

B. Well, congratulations! I'm very glad to hear that.

A. I have some good news.

B. What is it?

A. I just got a big raise!

B. You DID?!

A. Yes, I did.

B. I don't believe it! You didn't REALLY get a big raise, did you?

A. Yes, it's true. I DID.

B. Well, congratulations! I'm very glad to hear that!

1. I'm going to have a baby!

2. We won the basketball championship!

3. I've been promoted!

4. I can tie my shoes by myself!

5. My son is going to be in the Olympics!

6. I got a perfect score on the SAT test!

7. Steven Steelberg wants me to star in his new movie!

8. I've been invited to perform at the White House!

9. I was interviewed by *Time* Magazine yesterday!

10. My daughter has been accepted at Harvard University!

11. I've discovered a cure for the common cold!

12.

You're Right!

George was angry.	George **WAS** angry, wasn't he!
I'm late.	I **AM** late, aren't I!
They aren't very friendly.	They **AREN'T** very friendly, are they!
I don't know the answer.	I **DON'T** know the answer, do I!
They work hard.	They **DO** work hard, don't they!
John looks tired.	John **DOES** look tired, doesn't he!
Janet came late to class.	Janet **DID** come late to class, didn't she!

A. You know . . . the color blue looks very good on you.

B. You're right! The color blue DOES look very good on me, doesn't it!

A. You know . . . it isn't a very good day to fly a kite.

B. You're right! It ISN'T a very good day to fly a kite, is it!

1. . . . you work too hard.

2. . . . Charlie is a very talented dog.

3. . . . Aunt Betty hasn't called in a long time.

4.  . . . you're playing this song too slowly.

5.  . . . this milk tastes sour.

6.  . . . these hamburgers are overcooked.

7.  . . . you have quite a few gray hairs.

8.  . . . you've been online for a long time.

9.  . . . we really shouldn't be playing frisbee here.

10.  . . . Peter looks just like his father.

11.  . . . children these days don't dress very neatly.

12.  . . . you missed a few spots.

13.  . . . Ms. Taylor gave us a lot of homework yesterday.

14.  . . . I won't be able to play in the game tomorrow.

15.  . . . your brother and my sister would make a nice couple.

16.  . . . this new toaster doesn't work very well.

17.  . . . Howard was a very generous person.

18.

137

A BROKEN ENGAGEMENT

Dear John,

It's been a long time since I've written to you, hasn't it! I'm sorry it has taken me such a long time to write, but I really don't know where to begin this letter. You see, John, things have been very difficult since you took that job overseas several months ago. It has been very difficult for me to be engaged to somebody who is four thousand miles away, so I've decided that things have got to change.

I've decided to move out of my parents' house.

I'm going to get my own apartment.

I've started dating other guys.

I want to break our engagement.

And I gave your mother back the ring you had given me.

I'm sorry things have to end this way. You DO understand why I must do this, don't you?

Sincerely,
Jane

Dear Jane,

I received your letter today, and when I opened it I was shocked. I couldn't believe what you had written.

You haven't really decided to move out of your parents' house, have you?

You aren't really going to get your own apartment, are you?

You haven't really started dating other guys, have you?

You don't really want to break our engagement, do you?

And you didn't really give my mother back the ring I had given you, did you?

Please answer me as soon as possible!

Love,
John

P.S. You DO still love me, don't you?

Dear John,

    I HAVE decided to move out of my parents' house.

    I AM going to get my own apartment.

    I HAVE started dating other guys.

    I DO want to break our engagement.

    And I DID give your mother back the ring you had given me.

    I know this must hurt, but I DO have to be honest with you, don't I! I hope that someday you will understand.

            Good-bye,
            Jane

 READING *CHECK-UP*

WHAT'S THE ANSWER?

1. Why did Jane decide to break her engagement to John?
2. Where has Jane been living?
3. What did Jane do with the ring that John had given her?
4. How did John feel when he received Jane's first letter?
5. Did Jane realize how John would feel when he received her second letter?

CHOOSE

1. John wanted to know if Jane _____ to break their engagement.
   a. had really decided
   b. has really decided

2. John asked Jane whether she _____ her own apartment.
   a. had really gotten
   b. was really going to get

3. In her first letter, Jane said she _____ break their engagement.
   a. wants to
   b. wanted to

4. John was hoping she _____ him.
   a. still loved
   b. had still loved

5. In Jane's second letter, she told John she really _____ to move out of her parents' house.
   a. has decided
   b. had decided

6. She told him she hoped that someday he _____.
   a. would have understood
   b. would understand

IN YOUR OWN WORDS

FOR WRITING AND DISCUSSION

John is willing to do anything he can to save his relationship with Jane. He has some ideas about how to do this, and he's going to write to her one more time. Write John's letter to Jane.

UNFAIR ACCUSATIONS

```
To:   Michael Parker
From: Ms. Lewis
Re:   Your performance at work

I'm concerned about your performance at work.

    You have been working too slowly.
    You often get to work late.
    You took too many vacation days last month.
    You aren't very polite to the customers.
    And you don't get along well with the other employees.

I'd like to meet with you as soon as possible to discuss this.
```

Michael's boss, Ms. Lewis, sent him a memo recently about his performance at work. In the memo, she said he had been working too slowly. She also said that he often got to work late. In addition, she observed that he had taken too many vacation days last month. She also mentioned that he wasn't very polite to the customers. And finally, she complained that he didn't get along well with the other employees.

When Michael got the memo, he was very upset. He feels that his boss is making unfair accusations. Michael feels that he HASN'T been working too slowly. He also feels that he DOESN'T often get to work late. In Michael's opinion, he DIDN'T take too many vacation days last month. He thinks he IS very polite to the customers. And he maintains that he DOES get along well with the other employees.

Michael realizes that he and his boss see things VERY differently, and he plans to speak to her about this as soon as possible.

✔️ READING CHECK-UP

MATCH

Match the descriptions of job performance on the left with their meanings.

____ 1. punctual
____ 2. honest
____ 3. efficient
____ 4. industrious
____ 5. cooperative
____ 6. friendly
____ 7. considerate
____ 8. dedicated

a. pleasant and outgoing
b. easy to work with
c. works quickly and accurately
d. thoughtful of others
e. tells the truth
f. gets to work on time
g. cares about the work
h. works hard

LISTENING

Listen and decide who is speaking.

1. a. student – student
   b. student – teacher

2. a. tenant – tenant
   b. tenant – mail carrier

3. a. employee – employee
   b. student – student

4. a. salesperson – customer
   b. wife – husband

5. a. passenger – driver
   b. police officer – driver

6. a. doctor – nurse
   b. doctor – patient

IN YOUR OWN WORDS

FOR WRITING AND DISCUSSION

MEMO
To:
From:
Re:

Mr. Hopper is very pleased with Helen Baxter's performance at work. Using the story below as a guide, write a memo from Mr. Hopper to Helen Baxter.

POSITIVE FEEDBACK

Helen Baxter's boss, Mr. Hopper, sent her a memo recently about her job performance. He said that he was very pleased with her performance at work. He mentioned that she was very efficient and industrious. He observed that she got along well with her co-workers and customers. And he also said that she was very cooperative and considerate. Mr. Hopper wrote that the company had been so pleased with her work that they were going to give her a big raise.

141

INTERACTIONS

| He's / She's / It's } late, isn't { he! / she! / it! | We're / You're / They're } late, aren't { we! / you! / they! | I'm late, aren't I! |

A. You're tired, aren't you!

B. Tired? What makes you think I'm tired?

A. Well, you're falling asleep at the wheel.

B. Now that you mention it, I AM falling asleep at the wheel, aren't I!

A. You're nervous, aren't you!

B. Nervous? What makes you think I'm nervous?

A. Well, you haven't stopped pacing back and forth since early this morning.

B. Come to think of it, I HAVEN'T stopped pacing back and forth, have I!

A. You're in a bad mood, aren't you!

B. In a bad mood? What makes you think I'm in a bad mood?

A. Well, you shouted at me for no reason.

B. I guess I DID shout at you for no reason, didn't I!

142

A. You're _____, aren't you!

B. _____? What makes you think I'm _____?

A. Well, _____.

B. Now that you mention it,
Come to think of it,
I guess

_____, ____ ____!

Practice conversations with other students.

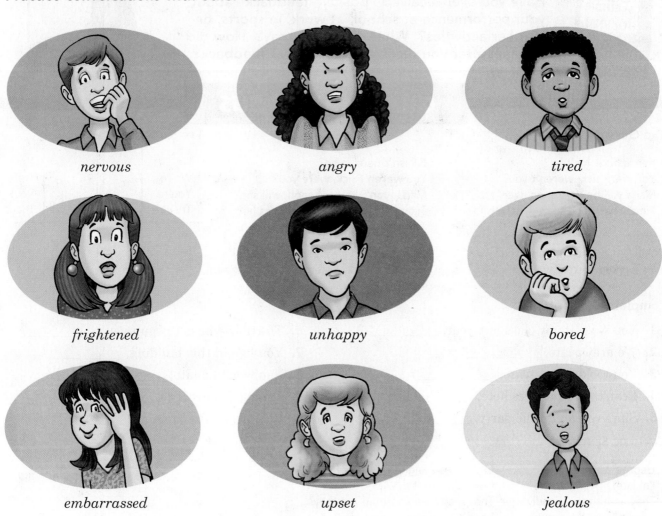

nervous

angry

tired

frightened

unhappy

bored

embarrassed

upset

jealous

How About You?

What do you do when you're nervous? angry? tired? frightened? unhappy? bored? embarrassed? upset? jealous?

PRONUNCIATION Tag Intonation

Listen. Then say it.

Ken is here, isn't he?

You weren't angry, were you?

They DO work hard, don't they!

They AREN'T friendly, are they!

Say it. Then listen.

Timmy has gone to bed, hasn't he?

They didn't leave, did they?

He DOESN'T know the answer, does he!

That WAS an awful movie, wasn't it!

Have you ever received "positive feedback" about your performance at school, at work, in sports, or in other activities? What did people say? How did you feel after you received the positive feedback?

GRAMMAR FOCUS

TAG QUESTIONS

Ken **is** here, **isn't** he?
You **were** sick, **weren't** you?
Maria **will** be here soon, **won't** she?
Timmy **has** gone to bed, **hasn't** he?

I **am** on time, **aren't** I?

You like ice cream, **don't** you?
Ed worked yesterday, **didn't** he?

Bill **isn't** here, **is** he?
You **weren't** sick, **were** you?
Maria **won't** be here soon, **will** she?
Timmy **hasn't** gone to bed, **has** he?

I'**m not** late, **am** I?

You **don't** like ice cream, **do** you?
Ed **didn't** work yesterday, **did** he?

TAG STATEMENTS

I'm We're You're They're	late,	aren't	I! we! you! they!
He's She's It's		isn't	he! she! it!

Complete the sentences.

1. You were in my class last year, _____ _____?

2. We aren't late, _____ _____?

3. You took the suitcases, _____ _____?

4. I can't take pictures here, _____ _____?

5. She's coming to the party, _____ _____?

6. The movie hasn't begun yet, _____ _____?

7. You live in this building, _____ _____?

8. You won't be late, _____ _____?

9. I'm not disturbing you, _____ _____?

10. I'm late for the meeting, _____ _____!

EMPHATIC SENTENCES

George was angry.	George WAS angry, wasn't he!
I'm late.	I AM late, aren't I!
They aren't very friendly.	They AREN'T very friendly, are they!
I don't know the answer.	I DON'T know the answer, do I!
They work hard.	They DO work hard, don't they!
John looks tired.	John DOES look tired, doesn't he!
Janet came late to class.	Janet DID come late to class, didn't she!

Complete the sentences.

11. These cookies are terrible! You're right. These cookies _____ terrible, _____ _____!

12. Cousin David hasn't called in a long time. You're right. He _____ called in a long time, _____ _____!

13. Our new sofa isn't very comfortable. You're right. Our new sofa _____ very comfortable, _____ _____!

14. Lisa looks like her mother. You're right. Lisa _____ look like her mother, _____ _____!

Review:
Verb Tenses
Conditionals
Gerunds

10

- Invitations
- Expressing Disappointment
- Calling Attention to People's Actions
- Apologizing
- Giving Reasons

- Decision-Making
- Consequences of Actions
- Expressing Concern About People
- Asking for Assistance

VOCABULARY PREVIEW

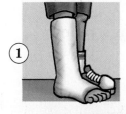 (1)
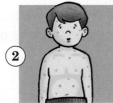 (2)
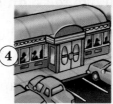 (3)
 (4)
 (5)

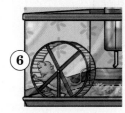 (6)
 (7)
 (8)
 (9)
 (10)

 (11)
 (12)
 (13)
 (14)
 (15)

1. cast
2. chicken pox
3. cockroach
4. diner
5. files

6. hamster
7. income tax return
8. key
9. mess
10. passport

11. pet food
12. satellite dish
13. scrap paper
14. wallpaper
15. wisdom tooth

Would You Like to Go on a Picnic with Me Today?

A. Would you like to **go on a picnic** with me today?

B. I don't think so. To be honest, I really don't feel like **going on a picnic** today. I **went on a picnic** yesterday.

A. That's too bad. I'm disappointed.

B. I hope you understand. If I hadn't **gone on a picnic** yesterday, I'd be very happy to **go on a picnic** with you today.

A. Of course I understand! After all, I suppose you'd get tired of **going on picnics** if you **went on picnics** all the time!

A. Would you like to _____ with me today?

B. I don't think so. To be honest, I really don't feel like _____ing today. I _____ yesterday.

A. That's too bad. I'm disappointed.

B. I hope you understand. If I hadn't _____ yesterday, I'd be very happy to _____ with you today.

A. Of course I understand! After all, I suppose you'd get tired of _____ing if you _____ all the time!

1. *see a movie*

2. *go to the mall*

3. *take a walk in the park*

4. *work out at the gym*

5. *go bowling*

6. *have lunch at Dave's Diner*

7. *drive around town*

8.

How to Say It!

Invitations

Would you like to
Do you want to } go on a picnic with me?
How would you like to

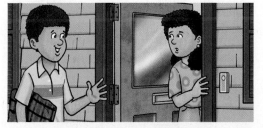

Practice the conversations in this lesson again. Invite people in different ways.

Do You Realize What You Just Did?!

A. Do you realize what you just did?!

B. No. What did I just do?

A. You just **ate both our salads**!

B. I did?

A. Yes, you did.

B. I'm really sorry. I must have **been very hungry**.
If I hadn't **been very hungry**, I NEVER would have **eaten both our salads**!

1. *throw out my homework*
think it was scrap paper

2. *drive past my house*
forget your address

3. *disconnect Aunt Thelma*
press the wrong button

4. *hit me with your umbrella*
be looking the other way

5. *step on my feet*
lose my balance

6. *give bird food to the hamster*
mix up the pet-food boxes

7. *paint the living room window*
have my mind on something else

8. *delete all my files*
hit the wrong key

9. *call me Gloria*
be thinking about somebody else

10. *put tomatoes in the onion soup*
misunderstand the recipe

11. *erase the video of my dance recital*
accidentally rewind the tape

12. *sit on my cat*
think it was a pillow

How About You?

Think of a time when you did something accidentally. What did you do? When did you realize what you had done? Why did it happen?

MARCIA'S BAD DAY

Marcia made several bad decisions yesterday.

She decided to drive to work, but she should have taken the train. If she had taken the train, she wouldn't have gotten stuck in a terrible traffic jam.

She decided to have lunch with a friend at a small restaurant far from her office, but she should have gone to a place nearby. If she had gone to a place nearby, she wouldn't have been an hour late for an important afternoon appointment.

She decided not to take the garbage out until after she got home from work that evening, but she should have taken it out in the morning. If she had taken it out in the morning, her cat wouldn't have tipped over the garbage pail and made such a mess in the kitchen.

And finally, that evening she decided to stay up late and watch a scary movie on TV, but she should have turned off the TV and gone to sleep. If she had turned off the TV and gone to sleep, she wouldn't have had terrible nightmares all night.

Marcia certainly didn't have a very good day yesterday. As a matter of fact, she probably shouldn't have gotten out of bed in the first place. If she hadn't gotten out of bed in the first place, none of this would ever have happened!

✔ READING CHECK-UP

TRUE, FALSE, OR MAYBE?

Answer True, False, or Maybe (if the answer isn't in the story).

1. Marcia wishes she hadn't taken the train to work yesterday.
2. If Marcia hadn't had lunch far from her office, she would have been on time for her appointment.
3. There aren't any small restaurants near Marcia's office.
4. She decided not to take the garbage out in the morning.
5. If Marcia hadn't watched a scary movie on TV, she probably wouldn't have had nightmares.

How About You?

We all sometimes make decisions we wish we hadn't made. Tell about some bad decisions you have made over the years. What did you decide to do? What should you have done? Why?

CHOOSE

1. If I _____ you were going to be in town, I would have invited you to stay with us.
   a. knew
   b. had known

2. If _____ busy tonight, I'll call you.
   a. I weren't
   b. I'm not

3. If I _____ the plane, I probably would have gotten there faster.
   a. had taken
   b. took

4. I _____ happy to go to the dance with you if you invited me.
   a. would be
   b. would have been

5. If I were you, I _____ that movie.
   a. wouldn't see
   b. won't see

6. I wish I _____ when I was young.
   a. learned to swim
   b. had learned to swim

7. If I had been more careful, I _____ driven through that stop sign.
   a. would have
   b. wouldn't have

8. I suppose you'd get tired of writing reports if you _____ reports all the time.
   a. wrote
   b. write

LISTENING

Listen and choose where the conversation is taking place.

1. a. restaurant
   b. someone's home

2. a. bus
   b. movie theater

3. a. park
   b. shopping mall

4. a. cafeteria
   b. supermarket

5. a. department store
   b. laundromat

6. a. airplane
   b. concert

You Seem Upset. Is Anything Wrong?

A. You seem upset. Is anything wrong?

B. Yes. **My computer is broken.**

A. I'm sorry to hear that. How long **has it been broken**?

B. **For two days.**

A. I know how upset you must be. I remember when **MY computer was broken.** Is there anything I can do to help?

B. Not really. But thanks for asking.

A. You seem upset. Is anything wrong?

B. Yes. _____.

A. I'm sorry to hear that. How long _____?

B. (For/Since) _____.

A. I know how upset you must be. I remember when

_____.

Is there anything I can do to help?

B. Not really. But thanks for asking.

1. My father is in the hospital.
   a week

2. My children have chicken pox.
   last Friday

3. The elevator in my building is out of order.
two weeks

4. My cat is lost.
three days

5. I'm unemployed.
March 1st

6. I'm having trouble sleeping at night.
a few weeks

7. Mr. Crump refuses to fix our bathtub.
a month

8. My wisdom teeth hurt.
Monday morning

9. My passport is missing.
I took an overnight train last week

10. The air conditioner in my office is broken.
the past week

11. I'm having trouble communicating with my children.
they became teenagers

12. My apartment has cockroaches.
a restaurant opened downstairs

Could You Possibly Come Over and Give Me a Hand?

A. Hello, Carlos? This is Gary.

B. Hi, Gary. How are you?

A. I'm okay. Listen, Carlos, I'm having trouble **putting up my satellite dish**. Could you possibly come over and give me a hand?

B. I'm really sorry, Gary. I'm afraid I can't come over right now. **I'm sick in bed.** If **I weren't sick in bed**, I'd be GLAD to help you put it up.

A. Don't worry about it. If I had known **you were sick in bed**, I wouldn't have called you in the first place!

A. Hello, _____? This is _____.

B. Hi, _____. How are you?

A. I'm okay. Listen, _____, I'm having trouble _____ing. Could you possibly come over and give me a hand?

B. I'm really sorry, _____. I'm afraid I can't come over right now.

_____.

If _____, I'd be GLAD to help you _____.

A. Don't worry about it. If I had known _____, I wouldn't have called you in the first place!

1. *hook up my DVD player*

2. *figure out the math homework*

3. *move my piano*

4. *assemble my new bookcases*

5. *fill out my income tax return*

6. *set up my new computer*

7. *replace the lock on my front door*

8. *program my new cell phone*

9. *pick out new wallpaper for my kitchen*

10.

DECISIONS

Several years ago, Stanley's friends urged him not to quit his job at the post office. They told him that if he quit his job there, he would never find a better one.

Stanley didn't follow their advice, and he's glad he didn't. He decided to quit his job at the post office, and he found work as a chef at a restaurant downtown. He saved all his money for several years, and then he opened a small restaurant of his own. Now his restaurant is famous, and people from all over town come to eat there.

Stanley is glad he didn't listen to his friends' advice. If he had listened to his friends' advice, he probably never would have opened his restaurant and become such a success.

Kelly's parents thought she was crazy when she bought a used car that had already been driven over two hundred thousand miles. They told her that if she bought that car, she'd probably have lots of problems with it.

Kelly didn't follow her parents' advice, and she's really sorry she didn't. Since she bought the car two months ago, she has had to take it to the garage for repairs seven times.

Kelly wishes she had listened to her parents. If she had listened to them, she never would have bought such a "lemon"!

Jason's ski instructor insisted that Jason wasn't ready to ski down the advanced slopes at the Magic Mountain ski resort. She told him that if he skied down the advanced slopes, he'd probably injure himself.

Jason didn't follow his ski instructor's advice, and he's very sorry he didn't. He skied down an advanced slope, and after just a few seconds, he fell and broke his leg.

Jason wishes he had listened to his ski instructor. If he had listened to her, he wouldn't be lying in the hospital with his leg in a cast.

✔ READING *CHECK-UP*

TRUE, FALSE, OR MAYBE?

Answer True, False, or Maybe (if the answer isn't in the story).

1. Stanley's friends thought he shouldn't continue working at the post office.
2. Stanley is glad he followed his friends' advice.
3. Kelly's mother and father never buy used cars.
4. Kelly's car has been at the garage for repairs for seven months.
5. If Jason had listened to his ski instructor's advice, he wouldn't have skied down an advanced slope.
6. Jason hasn't had his leg in a cast before.

CHOOSE

1. If he _____ to their advice, he wouldn't have gotten hurt.
    a. listened
    b. had listened

2. Since I bought this computer six weeks ago, _____ take it to the repair shop three times.
    a. I've had to
    b. I had to

3. I'm sorry I _____ to my parents' advice.
    a. didn't listen
    b. hadn't listened

4. Sarah wishes _____ bought a used car from Ralph Jones.
    a. she hasn't
    b. she hadn't

5. If I _____ have to work overtime today, I'd be glad to go to the concert with you.
    a. didn't
    b. don't

6. If I _____ sick, I'd be happy to come over and help you.
    a. wasn't
    b. weren't

PRONUNCIATION Would you & Could you

Listen. Then say it.

Would you like to see a movie?

How would you like to go dancing?

Could you possibly come over?

Say it. Then listen.

Would you like to have lunch?

How would you like to go bowling?

Could you possibly give me a hand?

SIDE by SIDE JOURNAL

Write in your journal about a time when you had to make an important decision and people gave you lots of advice. What was the situation? What did people tell you? Why did they tell you that? Did you follow their advice? What happened? Do you think you made the right decision? Why or why not?

GRAMMAR FOCUS

REVIEW OF VERB TENSES
PRESENT TENSE: TO BE

My computer **is** broken.

SIMPLE PAST

You just **ate** both our salads.

PRESENT CONTINUOUS

I**'m** hav**ing** trouble putting up my satellite dish.

PRESENT PERFECT

How long **has** it **been** broken?
It**'s been** broken for two days.

SIMPLE PRESENT

I don't feel like going on a picnic today.

CONDITIONALS: REVIEW

If I hadn't gone yesterday, I**'d** be very happy to go with you today.
If I hadn't been very hungry, I NEVER **would have** eaten both our salads!
If I had known you were sick in bed, I **wouldn't have** called you.

GERUNDS: REVIEW

I don't feel like **going** on a picnic today.
I suppose you'd get tired of **going** on picnics if you went on picnics all the time!

Choose the correct word.

1. If I (took   had taken) the train today, I (wouldn't have   had) gotten stuck in traffic, and I (would have arrived   would arrive) on time for work.

2. I don't feel like (to go   going) on a picnic today. I (went   have gone) on a picnic yesterday.

3. I'm sure I'd get tired (of jogging   to jog) if I (jog   jogged) all the time.

4. My daughter (has had   had) the measles since last weekend. I remember when I was a child and (have   had) the measles. I (hadn't   wasn't) ever been in bed for such a long time.

158

Feature Article
Fact File
Around the World
Interview
We've Got Mail!

SIDE *by* **SIDE** Gazette

Global Exchange
Listening
Fun with Idioms
What Are They
Saying?

Volume 4   Number 4

Technology in Our Lives

Technology plays a role in all aspects of our lives—the way we work, the way we shop, the way we communicate with each other, and the way we live at home. The speed of technological change in the past one hundred years has been incredible.

The early telephones were very large, and they didn't even have dials or buttons. You picked up a receiver and talked to an operator who made the call for you. Nowadays, cellular telephones fit in our pockets, and we can use them to make phone calls from anywhere to anywhere. In grocery stores and supermarkets, cashiers used to punch keys on cash registers to enter the price of each item. These days, scanners read bar codes on product packaging, and the prices are recorded by a computerized cash register. In some supermarkets, customers can even check out by scanning products themselves and paying by credit card, all without the help of a cashier. In the past, we made a trip to the bank to deposit or withdraw money. Now we can use ATMs (automated teller machines) that are found everywhere. And many people now do their bank transactions at home online over the Internet.

Modern technology has dramatically improved our lives. Personal computers enable us to create documents, store information, and analyze data—at work or at home. The Internet allows us to send and receive e-mail messages, connects us to the World Wide Web, and allows us to go shopping online from our homes. Digital cameras enable us to take photographs that we can instantly put on our computers to store, change, and send over the Internet. Satellite communication connects doctors in one country with a patient in another country, bringing medical technology to remote places

Telephones then and now

around the world. Miniature cameras that patients can swallow permit doctors to diagnose medical conditions without surgery. "Smart homes" operated by computers turn lights on and off as people enter or leave rooms and enable homeowners to "call their houses" to turn on the heat or air conditioning, or even to start the coffeemaker!

What will the future bring? "Smart highways" will carry us to destinations that we program into our cars' computers. Computer chips that are implanted under our skin will hold our medical information in case of an emergency. Household appliances, such as refrigerators and stoves, will have miniature computers that "know" how we like to store or cook our food.

Many people feel, however, that technology has its price. With automated supermarket checkout lines, ATMs and online banking, and Internet shopping, we can meet our daily needs without having contact with other people. Life with technology can be very lonely! Also, many people are concerned about privacy. Technology makes it possible for companies or the government to monitor our use of the Internet. Our credit card numbers, bank account information, medical information, and other personal data are all stored on computers. Protecting that information will be an important issue in the years ahead.

Banking then and now

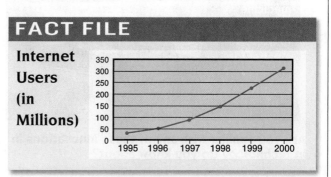
FACT FILE
Internet Users (in Millions)

Technology in Action

Innovations in technology are happening throughout the world.

A satellite dish provides television service to a village in Niger in Africa.

Computer technology developed in Tokyo, Japan scans people's eyes to verify their identity.

A new type of scanner screens the baggage of airline passengers at an airport in Washington, D.C.

Solar batteries provide electricity for a hospital in Sudan.

Business people in Sao Paulo, Brazil take part in a video conference with people at another location.

An on-board computer enables the driver of this car to get maps and other information over the Internet.

A doctor uses tele-medicine technology to examine a patient in another country.

A grandmother uses e-mail to keep in touch with her grandchildren who live far away.

Are you familiar with any of these innovations in technology? Which ones? What other innovations in technology do you know about?

Interview

A Side by Side Gazette reporter asked these people:

Q: How has technology changed your life?

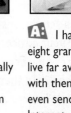

A: I use instant messaging all the time to stay in touch with my friends. I can have separate conversations with different friends at the same time over the Internet. It's better and cheaper than talking on the phone!

A: With today's computer and information technology, I don't have to go to my office every day. I "telecommute." I can connect to the computer network at my company and work from home.

A: I love my new game system! The graphics are amazing, and the action is really life-like! When I grow up, I want to develop game system software.

A: I have three children and eight grandchildren, and they all live far away. I keep in touch with them through e-mail. They even send me photos over the Internet. Technology keeps our family together.

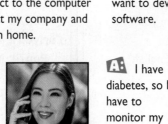

A: I don't know what I'd do without my cell phone! I'm never home, so I carry it with me everywhere. This way, my family and my friends can always reach me.

A: I have diabetes, so I have to monitor my blood sugar regularly. With my glucometer, I can check my blood sugar reading at any time of the day.

A: With my GPS device, I can navigate using global positioning satellite technology. It tells me the exact location of my boat at any moment.

FUN with IDIOMS

Do You Know These Expressions?

____ 1. There's a bug in this software!

____ 2. My computer has a virus!

____ 3. My computer is frozen!

____ 4. My computer is out of memory!

a. The system is infected.

b. There isn't space for more information.

c. The program has a problem.

d. Nothing is happening.

We've Got Mail!

Dear Side by Side,

    I have enjoyed using *Side by Side* in my English classes for the past two years. Now I'd like to ask for your advice. What is the best way for me to improve my English? Should I continue to study in school? Is there more grammar that I need to learn? What are some ways I can practice my English? I look forward to hearing from you.

Sincerely,
"Love Learning English"

Dear "Love Learning English,"

    We're happy to hear that you have been enjoying your English classes. In our opinion, you should definitely continue studying the language. There is more grammar to learn, and you will also be able to improve your listening, speaking, reading, and writing skills. In addition, try to use English as much as possible outside the classroom. Speak to people in English, watch English-language movies and TV shows, and try to communicate with people in English through letters or over the Internet. Thank you for writing, and good luck as you continue to study English!

Sincerely,
Side by Side

Global Exchange

Pop74:	Hi, Sally. This is Grandpa. What's new?
CurlyGirl:	NMU
Pop74:	?
CurlyGirl:	Not much. And you?
Pop74:	Grandma and I are fine. We loved the photos you sent us over the Internet of your Halloween party.
CurlyGirl:	THX
Pop74:	?
CurlyGirl:	Thanks.
Pop74:	You looked great in your bee costume. Did you sting anybody?
CurlyGirl:	LOL
Pop74:	?
CurlyGirl:	Laughing out loud.
Pop74:	Grandma says hello.
CurlyGirl:	G2G ILU
Pop74:	?
CurlyGirl:	Got to go. I love you.
Pop74:	ILU2

Have an instant message conversation with a keypal. Talk about anything you'd like. Use some abbreviations in your message.

MORE ABBREVIATIONS

WU? = What's up?	OIC = Oh, I see.
UW = You're welcome.	IMO = In my opinion
L8R = Later.	TTYL = Talk to you later.

LISTENING

Thank You for Calling the Service Department

These people are calling the service department of the Supersonic Electronics store. Which person is going to press each number?

  b   **1**   **a.** "When I try to play a video, nothing happens!"

  ___   **2**   **b.** "I don't hear any sound in my headphones!"

  ___   **3**   **c.** "Whenever I try to save my work, it freezes!"

  ___   **4**   **d.** "All my photographs are too dark!"

  ___   **5**   **e.** "I don't know how to record a message!"

  ___   **6**   **f.** "When I call people, I can hear them, but they can't hear me!"

What Are They Saying?

CHECK-UP TESTS
SKILLS CHECKS

Choose the correct answer.

1. I'm looking forward to attending my daughter's graduation _____.
   - Ⓐ competition
   - Ⓑ ceremony
   - Ⓒ composition
   - Ⓓ launch

2. Brenda recently spoke with the personnel officer of her company about her maternity _____.
   - Ⓐ celebration
   - Ⓑ job
   - Ⓒ leave
   - Ⓓ department

3. Oliver speaks with a British _____.
   - Ⓐ speech
   - Ⓑ system
   - Ⓒ accident
   - Ⓓ accent

4. My sister doesn't eat meat. She's been a _____ since she was in high school.
   - Ⓐ physician
   - Ⓑ veterinarian
   - Ⓒ vegetarian
   - Ⓓ couch potato

5. I'm sorry to hear you're sick. When did you _____ the flu?
   - Ⓐ come down with
   - Ⓑ come through
   - Ⓒ come over
   - Ⓓ come from

6. A. _____ a break yet?
   B. Yes. _____ a break a little while ago.
   - Ⓐ Did you take . . . I've taken
   - Ⓑ Have you taken . . . I took
   - Ⓒ Have you been taking . . . I took
   - Ⓓ Have you taken . . . I've been taking

7. A. _____ sailing recently?
   B. _____ sailing in a long time.
   - Ⓐ Did you go . . . I've gone
   - Ⓑ Have you gone . . . I didn't go
   - Ⓒ Have you gone . . . I haven't gone
   - Ⓓ Have you went . . . I haven't went

8. I'm very tired. _____ memos all morning. _____ more than 50.
   - Ⓐ I've been writing . . . I've written
   - Ⓑ I'm writing . . . I wrote
   - Ⓒ I wrote . . . I've been writing
   - Ⓓ I've written . . . I'm writing

9. _____ pancakes for breakfast yesterday. _____ pancakes the day before.
   - Ⓐ We had made . . . We didn't make
   - Ⓑ We haven't made . . . We made
   - Ⓒ We've made . . . We hadn't made
   - Ⓓ We didn't make . . . We had made

10. It's a shame I had to cancel my trip to London. _____ it for a long time.
    - Ⓐ I'm planning
    - Ⓑ I been planning
    - Ⓒ I had been planning
    - Ⓓ I had been planned

SKILLS CHECK

Match the "can do" statement and the correct sentence.

_____ 1. I can ask about skills.

_____ 2. I can tell about my work experience.

_____ 3. I can ask if actions have occurred.

_____ 4. I can tell about past activities.

_____ 5. I can ask about the duration of an activity.

_____ 6. I can tell about the duration of an activity.

_____ 7. I can express surprise.

_____ 8. I can describe the consequences of being late.

a. I went to the post office a little while ago.

b. I've been waiting for the bus since 8 o'clock.

c. Can you sing?

d. That's amazing!

e. Have you eaten lunch yet?

f. By the time I got to the bank, it had already closed.

g. I've driven trucks for many years.

h. How long have you been studying?

Choose the correct answer.

1. You need to get a good night's ____ before tomorrow's important test.
   - Ⓐ dream
   - Ⓑ oversleep
   - Ⓒ dinner
   - Ⓓ sleep

2. When the president came into the room, he ____ everybody's hand.
   - Ⓐ skipped
   - Ⓑ shook
   - Ⓒ shoveled
   - Ⓓ stood

3. I'm sorry I forgot to call you. I ____ you an apology.
   - Ⓐ owe
   - Ⓑ return
   - Ⓒ give
   - Ⓓ tell

4. My husband and I had some ____ problems last month and we weren't able to pay our rent on time.
   - Ⓐ expensive
   - Ⓑ pessimistic
   - Ⓒ final
   - Ⓓ financial

5. My children get frightened whenever they see a ____ movie.
   - Ⓐ scared
   - Ⓑ scary
   - Ⓒ mean
   - Ⓓ disappointed

6. I made a mistake. I ____ driven to work today. I ____ taken the bus instead.
   - Ⓐ shouldn't have . . . should have
   - Ⓑ should have . . . must have
   - Ⓒ may have . . . shouldn't have
   - Ⓓ must have . . . couldn't have

7. I wonder why our supervisor was an hour late for work today. She ____ the bus.
   - Ⓐ may miss
   - Ⓑ should miss
   - Ⓒ might have missed
   - Ⓓ mustn't have missed

8. I was sorry I tried to move my piano by myself. I'm very lucky. I ____ hurt my back.
   - Ⓐ shouldn't have
   - Ⓑ must have
   - Ⓒ could have
   - Ⓓ might

9. Our teacher didn't come to class today. She ____ do something very important.
   - Ⓐ should have had to
   - Ⓑ might have
   - Ⓒ shouldn't have to
   - Ⓓ must have had to

10. A. Tom looks exhausted. He ____ very far.
    B. He ____ jogged far, but that doesn't usually make him so exhausted.
    - Ⓐ must have jogged . . . might have
    - Ⓑ should have jogged . . . couldn't have
    - Ⓒ might jog . . . mustn't have
    - Ⓓ may have jogged . . . should have

SKILLS CHECK ✓

Match the "can do" statement and the correct sentence.

____ 1. I can evaluate people's activities.
____ 2. I can evaluate my own activities.
____ 3. I can express possibility.
____ 4. I can express uncertainty.
____ 5. I can express agreement.
____ 6. I can start a conversation.
____ 7. I can make a deduction.
____ 8. I can apologize.

a. I shouldn't have driven to work today.
b. I'm sorry.
c. Maybe you're right.
d. He should have driven more carefully.
e. He must have overslept.
f. I'm not sure.
g. If you ask me, . . .
h. She might have gone to the bank.

Choose the correct answer.

1. I recently _____ for a position at the Blackwell Company.
   - Ⓐ installed
   - Ⓑ adjusted
   - Ⓒ applied
   - Ⓓ considered

2. I hear they're going to _____ the factory that was destroyed by a fire last year.
   - Ⓐ rebuild
   - Ⓑ reject
   - Ⓒ compose
   - Ⓓ offer

3. Are you free now, Charlie? The mail needs to be _____.
   - Ⓐ invited
   - Ⓑ promoted
   - Ⓒ distributed
   - Ⓓ dedicated

4. Someone stole my wallet. All my money and _____ cards were taken.
   - Ⓐ construction
   - Ⓑ identification
   - Ⓒ information
   - Ⓓ invention

5. Do you think camping should be _____ in our city's public parks?
   - Ⓐ permitted
   - Ⓑ presented
   - Ⓒ conquered
   - Ⓓ received

6. A. Who _____ this picture?
   B. I'm pretty sure it _____ by your father.
   - Ⓐ was taken . . . took
   - Ⓑ took . . . was took
   - Ⓒ has taken . . . is being taken
   - Ⓓ took . . . was taken

7. You don't need to do the dishes. _____
   - Ⓐ They're did.
   - Ⓑ They've been done.
   - Ⓒ Their being done.
   - Ⓓ They've been did.

8. Mike _____ during a hockey game last night. That's the third time _____ this year.
   - Ⓐ has been hurt . . . he was hurt
   - Ⓑ was being hurt . . . he hurt
   - Ⓒ has hurt . . . he's being hurt
   - Ⓓ was hurt . . . he's been hurt

9. _____ by the bank in March and two months later _____ a raise.
   - Ⓐ I was hired . . . I was given
   - Ⓑ I've been hired . . . I gave
   - Ⓒ I was being hired . . . I've been given
   - Ⓓ I had hired . . . I'm being given

10. A. I'm calling about my TV. _____ fixed yet?
    B. _____ fixed right now.
    - Ⓐ Is it being . . . It's been
    - Ⓑ Has it been . . . It's being
    - Ⓒ Has it . . . It was
    - Ⓓ Has it been being . . . It's

SKILLS CHECK ✓

Match the "can do" statement and the correct sentence.

_____ 1. I can express agreement.

_____ 2. I can express uncertainty.

_____ 3. I can offer to do something.

_____ 4. I can decline an offer to do something.

_____ 5. I can share information about a person.

_____ 6. I can react to good news.

_____ 7. I can react to bad news.

_____ 8. I can give historical information.

a. I'm happy to hear that!

b. Do you want me to sweep the floor?

c. Have you heard about Helen?

d. I'm not sure.

e. The building was destroyed by a fire in 1895.

f. That's terrible!

g. I think so, too.

h. No. Don't worry about it.

Choose the correct answer.

1. Can we _____ you at that phone number?
- Ⓐ require
- Ⓑ receive
- Ⓒ run into
- Ⓓ reach

2. Natasha _____ to find out soon if she's going to get a raise.
- Ⓐ wonders
- Ⓑ expects
- Ⓒ invents
- Ⓓ results

3. They told us a long story about their trip, but we don't remember many of the _____.
- Ⓐ positions
- Ⓑ conditions
- Ⓒ details
- Ⓓ decisions

4. We've been waiting very _____ for the doctor.
- Ⓐ perfectly
- Ⓑ permanently
- Ⓒ positively
- Ⓓ patiently

5. What is your _____ to the missing person?
- Ⓐ relationship
- Ⓑ registration
- Ⓒ recreation
- Ⓓ reception

6. I have no idea _____ about.
- Ⓐ what are they arguing
- Ⓑ what they arguing
- Ⓒ what they're arguing
- Ⓓ what arguing are they

7. A. When does the plane leave?
   B. I'm not sure _____.
- Ⓐ when does the plane leave
- Ⓑ when the plane leaves
- Ⓒ when the plane does leave
- Ⓓ when leaves the plane

8. Do you know _____ his arm?
- Ⓐ how George broke
- Ⓑ how did George break
- Ⓒ how George did break
- Ⓓ how did George broke

9. The librarian can tell you _____ in the library.
- Ⓐ is talking permitted
- Ⓑ whether is talking permitted
- Ⓒ if talking is permitted
- Ⓓ whether is permitted talking

10. A. Who is he and why did he call us?
   B. I don't know _____ or _____.
- Ⓐ who he is . . . why did he call us
- Ⓑ who is he . . . why he call us
- Ⓒ who is he . . . why he called us
- Ⓓ who he is . . . why he called us

SKILLS CHECK

Match the "can do" statement and the correct sentence.

_____ **1.** I can ask for information.

_____ **2.** I can say that I don't know something.

_____ **3.** I can apologize.

_____ **4.** I can express uncertainty.

_____ **5.** I can make a suggestion.

_____ **6.** I can say that I don't remember something.

_____ **7.** I can ask for medical advice.

_____ **8.** I can express concern about someone.

a. I'm not really sure.

b. Do you know what the homework assignment is?

c. Why don't you ask the cashier?

d. Poor Rosemary!

e. I'm wondering if I should go on a diet.

f. I'm sorry.

g. I don't know when the train leaves.

h. I've forgotten where the plane tickets are.

Choose the correct answer.

1. My doctor says it's important to be in good physical _____.
   - Ⓐ reaction
   - Ⓑ reason
   - Ⓒ access
   - Ⓓ condition

2. My friends have been _____ me to look for a better job.
   - Ⓐ accepting
   - Ⓑ improving
   - Ⓒ encouraging
   - Ⓓ wishing

3. Michael sold a lot of cars this year. He hopes he receives a large year-end _____.
   - Ⓐ bill
   - Ⓑ bonus
   - Ⓒ economy
   - Ⓓ refund

4. Billy _____ his chemistry class. When his parents found out, they were very upset.
   - Ⓐ skipped
   - Ⓑ slipped
   - Ⓒ stopped
   - Ⓓ dropped off

5. I'm very concerned about air _____.
   - Ⓐ collection
   - Ⓑ competition
   - Ⓒ environment
   - Ⓓ pollution

6. If _____ sunny this weekend, _____ a picnic in the park.
   - Ⓐ it might be . . . we might have
   - Ⓑ it's . . . we'll probably have
   - Ⓒ it'll be . . . we'll have
   - Ⓓ it'll might be . . . we'll might have

7. A. I hope our guests _____ on time.
   B. I _____, too.
   - Ⓐ arrive . . . hope not
   - Ⓑ will arrive . . . will hope
   - Ⓒ arrive . . . hope so
   - Ⓓ might arrive . . . hope also

8. If Kevin _____ harder, _____ better grades.
   - Ⓐ studied . . . he'd get
   - Ⓑ studies . . . he'd get
   - Ⓒ studied . . . he'll get
   - Ⓓ studies . . . he'd might get

9. If Tina _____ careless, _____ so many mistakes
   - Ⓐ were . . . she would make
   - Ⓑ weren't . . . she wouldn't make
   - Ⓒ is . . . she'll make
   - Ⓓ weren't . . . she would make

10. I hope _____ a raise soon. If I do, _____ move to a nicer apartment.
    - Ⓐ I might get . . . I'll able to
    - Ⓑ I'll get . . . I'm able to
    - Ⓒ I get . . . I'll be able to
    - Ⓓ I got . . . I'd be able to

SKILLS CHECK ✓

Match the "can do" statement and the correct sentence.

_____ 1. I can ask about future plans.

_____ 2. I can express uncertainty.

_____ 3. I can make a prediction.

_____ 4. I can ask for advice.

_____ 5. I can express hopes.

_____ 6. I can express agreement.

_____ 7. I can make a deduction.

a. If I feel better, I'll probably go to work.

b. I'm not sure.

c. I hope our team wins the game tomorrow.

d. She must like her job.

e. What are you going to do tomorrow?

f. Do you think I should put some more salt in the soup?

g. You're right.

Choose the correct answer.

1. Mrs. Gleason hopes her son doesn't _____ out of law school.
   Ⓐ go
   Ⓑ lose
   Ⓒ drop
   Ⓓ skip

2. I live in the suburbs and have to _____ into the city for work every day.
   Ⓐ concentrate
   Ⓑ convince
   Ⓒ move
   Ⓓ commute

3. If you don't pay your rent on time, there's a chance you'll be _____ from your apartment.
   Ⓐ evicted
   Ⓑ examined
   Ⓒ collected
   Ⓓ replaced

4. I'm having trouble with my Spanish pronunciation. I need to learn how to _____ my "Rs".
   Ⓐ return
   Ⓑ roll
   Ⓒ receive
   Ⓓ repeat

5. Fred can't fix anything around the house. Everybody tells him he's _____.
   Ⓐ sick and tired
   Ⓑ handy
   Ⓒ capable
   Ⓓ all thumbs

6. If I were you, _____ that hat. If you did, I think _____ it.
   Ⓐ I didn't buy . . . you regretted
   Ⓑ I won't buy . . . you'll regret
   Ⓒ I'm not buying . . . you're regretting
   Ⓓ I wouldn't buy . . . you'd regret

7. You and I are different. I wish _____ the day shift, and you wish _____ the night shift.
   Ⓐ I work . . . you work
   Ⓑ I worked . . . you work
   Ⓒ I worked . . . you worked
   Ⓓ I'm working . . . you're working

8. I wish _____ fix my car by myself. If I could, _____ save money on repairs.
   Ⓐ I'm able to . . . I'd be able to
   Ⓑ I were able to . . . I'd be able to
   Ⓒ was I able to . . . I'm able to
   Ⓓ I could . . . I'll be able to

9. I wish _____ on the first floor. If my apartment were on a higher floor, _____ a better view from my window.
   Ⓐ I didn't live . . . I'd have
   Ⓑ I don't live . . . I'll have
   Ⓒ I'm not living . . . I'm having
   Ⓓ I wasn't living . . . I'll be having

10. I wish the people in this neighborhood _____ friendlier. If they were friendlier, _____ looking for another place to live.
    Ⓐ were . . . I wouldn't be
    Ⓑ are . . . I won't be
    Ⓒ are . . . I'll be
    Ⓓ were . . . I'd wouldn't be

SKILLS CHECK ✓

Match the "can do" statement and the correct sentence.

_____ 1. I can ask for advice.
_____ 2. I can express certainty.
_____ 3. I can give advice.
_____ 4. I can give a personal opinion.
_____ 5. I can express agreement.
_____ 6. I can express wishes.
_____ 7. I can ask for a reason.

a. To be honest with you, . . .
b. I suppose you're right.
c. Why do you say that?
d. I'm positive.
e. I wouldn't get a dog if I were you.
f. I wish I were an actor.
g. Do you think the boss would be angry if I went home early?

Choose the correct answer.

1. I'm sure that my parents are ____ about my future.
   - Ⓐ advanced
   - Ⓑ concerned
   - Ⓒ approved
   - Ⓓ prepared

2. I got ____ by a security person after I went through the metal detector.
   - Ⓐ shrunk
   - Ⓑ transferred
   - Ⓒ put up
   - Ⓓ searched

3. We need to buy a few more of the ____ we need for this recipe.
   - Ⓐ instructions
   - Ⓑ decorations
   - Ⓒ ingredients
   - Ⓓ details

4. Everybody was impressed by the singer's magnificent ____.
   - Ⓐ performance
   - Ⓑ permission
   - Ⓒ environment
   - Ⓓ satisfaction

5. If I were an optimist, I wouldn't feel ____ so often.
   - Ⓐ impressed
   - Ⓑ depressed
   - Ⓒ expressed
   - Ⓓ confident

6. If Ronald's computer ____ working last night, ____ his paper on time today.
   - Ⓐ had been . . . he would have turned in
   - Ⓑ would be . . . he could turn in
   - Ⓒ was . . . he'll turn in
   - Ⓓ could be . . . he would turn in

7. If Julia ____ an unusually difficult day at work today, she ____ to sleep so early.
   - Ⓐ didn't have . . . wouldn't go
   - Ⓑ hadn't had . . . wouldn't have gone
   - Ⓒ hasn't had . . . hasn't gone
   - Ⓓ wasn't having . . . wouldn't go

8. I wish ____ the report was due yesterday. ____ it the night before.
   - Ⓐ I had known . . . I would have finished
   - Ⓑ I knew . . . I'd finish
   - Ⓒ I was knowing . . . I could finish
   - Ⓓ I've known . . . I've finished

9. Howard wishes ____ more often. If he did, he ____ go on a diet.
   - Ⓐ he's exercised . . . hasn't had to
   - Ⓑ he exercises . . . doesn't have to
   - Ⓒ he's exercising . . . didn't have to
   - Ⓓ he exercised . . . wouldn't have to

10. I wish ____ for my English test last night. If I had studied, I ____ such a bad grade.
    - Ⓐ I've studied . . . haven't gotten
    - Ⓑ I studied . . . wouldn't get
    - Ⓒ I had studied . . . wouldn't have gotten
    - Ⓓ I was studying . . . won't get

SKILLS CHECK ✓

Match the "can do" statement and the correct sentence.

____ 1. I can ask for a reason.
____ 2. I can make a deduction.
____ 3. I can express agreement.
____ 4. I can express a wish about something in the present.
____ 5. I can express a wish about something in the past.
____ 6. I can empathize.
____ 7. I can express hopes.

a. You're probably right.
b. I wish I had done my homework last night.
c. Why weren't you in class yesterday?
d. I know what you mean.
e. I wish I knew my neighbors.
f. He must have been in a hurry.
g. I hope it's a nice day tomorrow.

Choose the correct answer.

1. I'm confident that I'm _____ for the job at the Allied Insurance Company.
   - (A) successful
   - (B) positive
   - (C) hardworking
   - (D) qualified

2. Andrew and Susan recently got _____ to be married.
   - (A) exchanged
   - (B) engaged
   - (C) arranged
   - (D) decided

3. Our son-in-law has an important _____ at the bank.
   - (A) position
   - (B) location
   - (C) instruction
   - (D) promotion

4. The plumber is here. She needs to figure out what's _____ our pipes.
   - (A) composing
   - (B) crashing
   - (C) clogging
   - (D) collecting

5. Our daughter has been studying very hard for the college _____ exam.
   - (A) performance
   - (B) entrance
   - (C) information
   - (D) presentation

6. The repairperson called and said our computer _____ and _____ pick it up anytime.
   - (A) has been repaired . . . can we
   - (B) had been repaired . . . we could
   - (C) repaired . . . we can
   - (D) was repairing . . . could we

7. Everybody in the office is saying that the boss is leaving the company. I had no idea _____.
   - (A) was he leaving
   - (B) is he leaving
   - (C) he was leaving
   - (D) if he's leaving

8. I couldn't believe it! My girlfriend asked me _____ break up with her!
   - (A) I wanted to
   - (B) did I want to
   - (C) do I want to
   - (D) if I wanted to

9. My doctor told me _____ in bed and _____ anything spicy.
   - (A) rest . . . to not eat
   - (B) be resting . . . don't eat
   - (C) to rest . . . not to eat
   - (D) to be resting . . . not eat

10. My next-door neighbor told me _____ the piano any more. He said the noise _____ him.
    - (A) not to play . . . was bothering
    - (B) not play . . . bothers
    - (C) don't play . . . is bothering
    - (D) to don't play . . . bothered

SKILLS CHECK

Match the "can do" statement and the correct sentence.

_____ 1. I can report what people have said.

_____ 2. I can ask for information.

_____ 3. I can report information.

_____ 4. I can express surprise.

_____ 5. I can express feelings and emotions.

_____ 6. I can ask for a reason.

_____ 7. I can say that I didn't know about something.

a. I'm a little annoyed at my neighbors.

b. A lion has escaped from the zoo!

c. How come?

d. I didn't know that our English teacher was in the hospital.

e. She said that she was sick.

f. You've got to be kidding!

g. What's everybody talking about?

Choose the correct answer.

1. My son has his first job interview tomorrow morning. I told him that it's important to be _____.
   - ⒜ industrious
   - ⒝ punctual
   - ⒞ efficient
   - ⒟ personal

2. Everybody at the office likes and respects Janine. She always thinks of others. She's a kind, cooperative, and _____ person.
   - ⒜ considerate
   - ⒝ conservative
   - ⒞ convenient
   - ⒟ similar

3. I hope that some day a scientist discovers the _____ for the common cold.
   - ⒜ examination
   - ⒝ construction
   - ⒞ presentation
   - ⒟ cure

4. My supervisor sent me a memo recently. She said I had been working too slowly. I think that's an unfair _____.
   - ⒜ application
   - ⒝ decision
   - ⒞ accusation
   - ⒟ expression

5. I'm really sorry. Now that you _____ it, I guess I HAVE been in a bad mood recently, haven't I!
   - ⒜ advise
   - ⒝ mention
   - ⒞ receive
   - ⒟ suppose

6. A. The store hasn't closed yet, _____?
   B. Actually, _____.
   A. I'm surprised. I was sure it _____.
   - ⒜ has it . . . it has . . . hadn't
   - ⒝ has it . . . it hasn't . . . had
   - ⒞ hasn't it . . . it has . . . has
   - ⒟ hasn't it . . . it hasn't . . . hasn't

7. A. You're allergic to bees, _____?
   B. Actually, _____.
   A. Really? I was sure you _____.
   - ⒜ aren't you . . . I am . . . weren't
   - ⒝ aren't you . . . I'm not . . . were
   - ⒞ are you . . . I'm not . . . aren't
   - ⒟ are you . . . I am . . . are

8. A. I have some bad news. I got fired.
   B. You didn't really get fired, _____?
   A. It's true. I _____.
   - ⒜ didn't you . . . didn't
   - ⒝ didn't you . . . did
   - ⒞ did you . . . didn't
   - ⒟ did you . . . did

9. A. You know . . . you've been eating too many rich desserts recently.
   B. You're right! I _____ too many rich desserts, _____!
   - ⒜ AM eating . . . are I
   - ⒝ HAVE . . . have I
   - ⒞ HAVE been eating . . . haven't I
   - ⒟ DO eat . . . do I

10. A. The guests at our party aren't having a very good time.
    B. I know. They _____ a good time, _____!
    - ⒜ ARE having . . . are they
    - ⒝ DON'T have . . . don't they
    - ⒞ ARE having . . . are they
    - ⒟ AREN'T having . . . are they

SKILLS CHECK ✓

Match the "can do" statement and the correct sentence.

_____ 1. I can verify information.
_____ 2. I can express surprise.
_____ 3. I can share information.
_____ 4. I can congratulate someone.
_____ 5. I can initiate a topic of conversation.
_____ 6. I can describe feelings and emotions.
_____ 7. I can ask for a reason.

a. Congratulations!
b. You're nervous, aren't you!
c. I can't believe it!
d. This is the bus to the zoo, isn't it?
e. What makes you think I'm tired?
f. I have some good news.
g. You know . . .

Choose the correct answer.

1. I turned left at the light and got completely lost. I must have _____ the directions.
   - Ⓐ understood
   - Ⓑ mixed
   - Ⓒ misunderstood
   - Ⓓ figured out

2. It's very easy to use this new phone. _____ this button to make a call.
   - Ⓐ Rewind
   - Ⓑ Disconnect
   - Ⓒ Delete
   - Ⓓ Press

3. Roger hurt himself while he was skiing. He shouldn't have been skiing on the advanced _____.
   - Ⓐ slopes
   - Ⓑ slips
   - Ⓒ scraps
   - Ⓓ stops

4. The cat _____ the garbage pail in the kitchen and it made a big mess. I'll clean it up.
   - Ⓐ hooked up
   - Ⓑ tripped
   - Ⓒ tipped over
   - Ⓓ overcooked

5. Do you think you'd be able to help me _____ my new laptop sometime this afternoon?
   - Ⓐ mix up
   - Ⓑ set up
   - Ⓒ look up
   - Ⓓ develop

6. My friend asked me to see a movie today, but _____ a movie yesterday. If I _____ a movie yesterday, I'd be happy to see one today.
   - Ⓐ I've seen . . . haven't seen
   - Ⓑ I had seen . . . didn't see
   - Ⓒ I saw . . . wasn't seeing
   - Ⓓ I saw . . . hadn't seen

7. I'm sorry I spilled coffee on your rug. If I _____ daydreaming, I never _____ that.
   - Ⓐ wasn't . . . did
   - Ⓑ weren't . . . had done
   - Ⓒ haven't been . . . have done
   - Ⓓ hadn't been . . . would have done

8. I shouldn't have ordered the fish. If _____ ordered something else, I _____ sick.
   - Ⓐ I had . . . wouldn't have gotten
   - Ⓑ I . . . won't get
   - Ⓒ I've . . . won't have gotten
   - Ⓓ I . . . wouldn't get

9. I'm really sorry. If _____ busy, I wouldn't _____ you to help me today.
   - Ⓐ I've known you're . . . had asked
   - Ⓑ I knew you're . . . ask
   - Ⓒ I had known you were . . . have asked
   - Ⓓ I know you were . . . have asked

10. I glad I didn't follow my friends' advice. If _____ their advice, I _____ to medical school and become a doctor.
    - Ⓐ I followed . . . didn't go
    - Ⓑ I had followed . . . wouldn't have gone
    - Ⓒ I would follow . . . wouldn't go
    - Ⓓ I've followed . . . haven't gone

SKILLS CHECK ✓

Match the "can do" statement and the correct sentence.

_____ 1. I can invite someone to do something.

_____ 2. I can express feelings and emotions.

_____ 3. I can tell about the consequences of actions.

_____ 4. I can call attention to a person's actions.

_____ 5. I can apologize.

_____ 6. I can make a deduction.

_____ 7. I can express concern about someone.

a. If I hadn't gone on a picnic yesterday, I'd be happy to go on a picnic today.
b. I must have been very hungry.
c. I'm disappointed.
d. You seem upset. Is anything wrong?
e. Would you like to see a movie with me today?
f. I'm sorry.
g. Do you realize what you just did?

APPENDIX

Listening Scripts

Chapter 1 – Page 6

Carl is going to have a party at his apartment this Saturday night. This is the list of things that Carl needs to do to get ready for his party. Check the things on the list that Carl has already done.

Carl has already gone to the supermarket. He hasn't cleaned the apartment yet. He also hasn't gotten balloons at the party store. He's bought some new dance music at his favorite CD store. He hasn't hung up the decorations yet. He also hasn't made the food. He has told the neighbors about the party so they won't be surprised when they hear the noise. He'll give the dog a bath a few hours before the party begins.

Chapter 2 – Page 19

Listen and choose the best answer based on the conversation you hear.

1. A. By the time we got to the party, everyone had left.
   B. That's too bad.
2. A. I couldn't hear a word he said.
   B. I couldn't either.
3. A. I just interviewed a young man for the bookkeeper's position.
   B. What did you think of him?
   A. Well, he was very shy and quiet, and he was wearing a T-shirt, jeans, and sneakers.
4. A. Could you tell me how I did on the exam?
   B. Not very well, Richard.
5. A. I smell smoke!
   B. Oh, no! The cookies are burning!
6. A. I was so tired last night that I slept twelve hours and was late for work this morning.
   B. Oh. I hope the boss wasn't angry.
   A. No. He wasn't.

Chapter 3 – Page 42

Listen and choose the best line to continue the conversation.

1. The packages have been sent.
2. The beds have been made.
3. Our cat was bitten by our dog.
4. My brother was invited to his girlfriend's birthday party.
5. Mrs. Green hired Mr. Fleming as a secretary.
6. Mrs. Davis was hired by Ms. Clark to work in the information technology department.
7. Hello. This is the Worldcom Service Department. Your cell phone has been repaired.
8. Hello. This is Joe's Auto Repair Shop. I'm sorry. We've been very busy. I'm calling to tell you your car is finally being repaired.

Side by Side Gazette – Page 50

Listen to the news reports. Answer true or false.

Good afternoon. This is Gloria Ramos in the WKSB radio newsroom with the latest news update. A bicyclist was knocked down in a hit-and-run accident on Jefferson Street this afternoon. A brown van was seen leaving the scene of the accident. If you have any information, the police department is asking you to call 555-1234. Live in the newsroom, this is Gloria Ramos for WKSB Radio News.

This is Kim Crane reporting live from City Hall. A new mayor has been elected. It was a very close race between Joe Murphy and Julie Miller, but now the results are in, and Julie Miller has been chosen as the new mayor. Julie Miller will be interviewed on this evening's news at six o'clock.

This is Stu Brent reporting live from downtown. I'm at the scene of the big fire at the Main Street Marketplace. Five stores at the Marketplace were destroyed in this fire that broke out early this morning. Luckily, no one was injured. The building is now being examined by the fire department. The fire chief is expected to speak at a news conference later this afternoon. We'll bring that news conference to you live when it happens.

This is Brian Adams with a local sports update. After five years as the city's baseball champions, the Washington High School Eagles were defeated by the Lincoln High School Terriers this afternoon by a score of 4 to 3. The Terriers are the new baseball champions. Tune in at 5 o'clock for the complete story.

This is Wendy Chen reporting live from the Museum of Fine Arts. Last night, the museum was robbed, and several important paintings were stolen. The paintings are considered some of the best works by painters known throughout the world, including Picasso, Rembrandt, and Monet. The robbery was discovered this morning when the museum's director arrived for work. The building is now being checked by the police, and information about the missing paintings is being sent around the nation and around the world. Reporting live from the Museum of Fine Arts, this is Wendy Chen for KPLW Radio News.

Chapter 4 – Page 61

Listen and decide where the conversation is taking place.

1. A. Could you please tell me if this book is on sale?
   B. Yes, it is.
2. A. Can you tell me where the bananas are?
   B. Yes. They're in the next aisle.
   A. Thanks very much.
3. A. Do you know how much this shirt costs?
   B. I'm sorry. I don't work here.
4. A. Do you know who composed this symphony?
   B. I think Beethoven did.
5. A. Do you by any chance know whether we'll be arriving soon?
   B. Yes. We'll be arriving in ten minutes.
   A. Thank you.
6. A. Who knows how a heart works?
   B. I do.
   A. Please tell us.
7. A. Do you know how much longer I'll have to stay here?
   B. Just a few more days.
   A. Oh, good.
8. A. Do you have any idea when the bus from Detroit arrives?
   B. I'm not sure. You should ask the man at the ticket counter. He'll know when the bus arrives.

Chapter 5 – Page 76

Listen and choose the statement that is true based on what you hear.

1. If it weren't raining today, we'd go to the beach.
2. If we had enough money, we'd buy a new car.
3. I'd be very happy if Mrs. Carter were my English teacher.
4. If the company's profits increase, we'll receive bonuses.
5. If I weren't allergic to trees, I'd go hiking with you this weekend.
6. If I didn't have to work tonight, I'd invite you to go to the movies with me.

Side by Side Gazette – Page 82

Listen to the Tempo Airlines automated telephone system. Match the numbers and the menu instructions.

Thank you for calling Tempo Airlines—the airline that puts passengers first! This call may be monitored to ensure quality assistance. Please listen carefully to the following menu:

If you are calling for information about today's flights, press 1.

If you are calling to make a reservation for a flight in the United States or Canada, press 2.

If you are calling to make a reservation for an international flight, press 3.

If you are calling to make a reservation for a Tempo Airlines Vacation Package, press 4.

If you are calling to enroll in the Tempo Airlines Frequent Flyer Program, which gives you awards for all travel on Tempo Airlines, press 5.

If you want to hear a list of rules for checking in at the airport, press 6.

If you want to speak with a customer service representative, press 7.

To hear this menu again, press 8.

If you are not calling from a touch-tone phone, please stay on the line and a Tempo Airlines representative will be with you shortly. Thank you for choosing Tempo Airlines.

Chapter 6 – Page 93

Listen and choose the statement that is true based on what you hear.

1. If I got a dog, I'd probably be evicted from my apartment building.
2. I wish I worked the day shift.
3. If I weren't a teacher, I'd probably be a musician.
4. I wish I didn't have to take biology next semester.
5. If I could type fast, I'd be able to get a better job.
6. If they lived in the city, they'd be able to sell their car.

Chapter 7 – Page 105

Listen and choose the statement that is true based on what you hear.

1. A. If I were rich, I'd travel around the world.
   B. Really? That sounds like fun!

2. A. Why didn't you e-mail me?
   B. I would have e-mailed you if I hadn't forgotten your e-mail address.

3. A. How did you enjoy the soccer game?
   B. It was all right, but I wish we could have had better seats.

4. A. Those boys are making a lot of noise in the hallway again.
   B. I know. It's terrible. If they weren't the landlord's children, I'd tell them to be quiet.

5. A. You know, I wish I had taken a computer course when I was in college.
   B. Why do you say that?
   A. If I had, I would have gotten the job I applied for.

6. A. Happy Birthday, Johnny! Now blow out the candles and make a wish.
   B. I wish Grandma and Grandpa were here for my birthday party.

Chapter 8 – Page 115

Listen and choose the statement that is true based on what you hear.

1. A. I've been in the office all day. I wasn't aware that it had snowed.
   B. I wasn't either.

2. A. Have you heard the news?
   B. No. What?
   A. Our supervisor is in the hospital.
   B. Oh. I didn't know that. That's too bad.

3. A. Do you know about the special sale?
   B. No, I don't.
   A. You can buy two jackets for the price of one this week.
   B. No kidding! That's great!

4. A. Hello.
   B. Hello, Tim? This is Barbara. I'm afraid I won't be able to have dinner with you on Saturday. I have to work.
   A. Oh. That's too bad.

5. A. Sherman quit his job!
   B. Really? What a surprise!

6. A. We've moved!
   B. Oh. I didn't know that. Where to?
   A. The other side of the town.

Side by Side Gazette – Page 128

Joe Montero is the office manager at his company. Listen to his voice mail messages. Why did each person call?

You have six messages.

Message Number One: "Hello. This is Jim Gavin. I'm one of the new employees on the third floor. I have a question. Why was three hundred and fifty dollars taken out of my paycheck? If you have time today, could you please call me at extension 45? Thanks very much." [*beep*]

Message Number Two: "Hi. This is Denise. I'm sorry, but I won't be able to go to the meeting this afternoon. I just found out about the meeting a half hour ago, and I have to pick up the boss at the airport. Let me know how the meeting goes." [*beep*]

Message Number Three: "Hi, Joe. This is Patty in Accounting. I see that you've just ordered one thousand pens for the office. I'm calling to let you know that we still have enough pens from our last order, so we won't need any more pens for a few more months. I've canceled the order. Okay? Thanks." [*beep*]

Message Number Four: "Hello. This is Jane Adams calling from the president's office. You told me yesterday that the painters would begin painting the president's office today, but they haven't arrived yet. Please let me know when they'll be here. Thank you." [*beep*]

Message Number Five: "Hello. This is George Johnson. I wanted to let you know that I won't be in the office tomorrow morning. I have to go to a doctor's appointment. If you need to talk to me, you can reach me on my cell phone at 881-595-7472. Thanks." [*beep*]

Message Number Six: "Joe? This is Michelle Mills. I really need to talk with you as soon as possible. I've been offered a job at another company, and I don't know what to do. I'd really like to stay here, but they're offering me a job with more responsibilities and a higher salary. Please call me back so we can set up a time to meet. Thanks." [*beep*]

Chapter 9 – Page 141

Listen and decide who is speaking.

1. A. I did well on my exam, didn't I?
   B. No, you didn't.
   A. I didn't?! I'm really surprised.

2. A. The mail isn't here yet, is it?
   B. No. Not yet.
   A. That's what I thought.

3. A. You've received our supervisor's memo, haven't you?
   B. Yes, I have.

4. A. You know . . . that suit looks very good on you.
   B. You're right! It DOES look very good on me, doesn't it!
   A. Yes, it does. I wonder if it's on sale.
   B. Let's ask somebody.

5. A. You were driving more than seventy miles per hour, weren't you!
   B. I guess I was. Are you going to give me a ticket?

6. A. I have some good news!
   B. What is it?
   A. You're fine. You can go home tomorrow.
   B. I can?!
   A. Yes, you can.
   B. I'm very glad to hear that.

Chapter 10 – Page 151

Listen and choose where the conversation is taking place.

1. A. Do you realize what you just did?
   B. No. What did I just do?
   A. You put too much pepper in the soup. Our customers will be sneezing all night!
   B. Oh. I'm sorry. I must have had my mind on something else.

2. A. I'm sorry. I must have thought this seat was mine.
   B. That's okay. Don't worry about it. I'm getting off soon anyway.

3. A. You know, I really don't feel like shopping today. Could we go someplace else and take a walk?
   B. Sure. That's fine with me.

4. A. What are you going to have?
   B. I'm not sure. If I hadn't had the chicken every day last week, I'd have the chicken.

5. A. Excuse me. You just put my shirts in your machine.
   B. I did?
   A. Yes, you did.
   B. I'm really sorry. I thought they were mine.

6. A. If I had known this was going to be so boring, I wouldn't have bought a ticket.
   B. I agree. I wouldn't have bought one either.

Side by Side Gazette – Page 162

These people are calling the service department of the Supersonic Electronics store. Listen to the service department's automated telephone system. Which person is going to press each number?

Thank you for calling the Supersonic Electronics Service Department. Our menu has changed, so please listen carefully to the following options:

If you are calling about a personal audio device such as a portable CD player, press 1.

If your call is related to a VCR or DVD player, press 2.

If you need assistance with a digital camera or video camcorder, press 3.

If this call is about a cellular phone, press 4.

If you are having a problem with a desktop computer or a notebook computer, press 5.

If you are calling about a telephone answering machine, press 6.

If you would like to speak to a customer service representative, press 7.

If you would like to hear these menu options again, press 8.

To end this call, please hang up.

Thank you for calling the Supersonic Electronics Service Department.

Thematic Glossary

Actions and Activities

abandon 48
adjust 42
advise 122
agree 57
allow 43
amaze 47
analyze 159
answer 57
answer the phone 15
apologize 15
apply 39
appreciate 79
approve 97
argue 7
arrest 117
arrive 18
ask 6
assassinate 57
assemble 8
attack 45
attend 44
award 47
baby-sit 111
bake 101
bark 75
be born 49
beat 127
begin 11
believe 9
bite 28
blow 13
blow away 13
blow out 80
borrow 85
bother 76
brag 125
break 20
break into 77
break out 44
break up 12
bring 50
build 9
bury 48
buy 6
call 40
call back 114
cancel 12
capture 45
care 73
carry 159
catch 22
cause 28
celebrate 134
change 42
charge 42
check 42
check in 82
check out 159
check with 54
choose 37
clean 6
clip 41
clog 121
close 11
close down 104
come 20
come back 20
come down with 12
come over 154
come true 80
communicate 29

commute 92
complain 140
complete 44
compose 32
concentrate 91
connect 48
conquer 45
consider 44
construct 47
contact 125
continue 157
contribute 127
convince 90
cook 17
cost 53
create 47
cry 52
dance 7
date 138
daydream 15
deal with 125
decide 13
dedicate 48
defeat 50
delete 149
deliver 9
depend 122
deposit 159
describe 125
design 33
destroy 44
develop 47
diagnose 159
die 48
direct 33
disconnect 148
discover 45
discuss 140
distribute 35
disturb 121
do 1
do over 121
do sit-ups 1
draw 2
dress up 65
dress 19
drive 1
drop 70
drop in 65
drop out 85
drown 22
dye 118
eat 1
elect 50
employ 125
enable 159
encourage 49
end 11
enjoy 87
enlarge 48
enroll 82
ensure 82
enter 159
entertain 48
erase 149
erect 48
escape 113
establish 47
estimate 48
evict 28
exaggerate 127
examine 50
exercise 73

expect 50
explain 82
explore 49
express 79
fail 15
faint 127
fall asleep 142
fall down 13
fall in love 111
fall through 22
feed 3
feel 13
figure out 155
fill 79
fill out 101
find 33
find out 128
finish 11
fire 28
fish 131
fit 159
fix 41
fly 2
focus 50
follow 48
forget 20
found 45
get 1
get accepted 71
get along with 73
get depressed 103
get laid off 12
get lost 15
get married 13
get paid 73
get scared 28
get searched 99
get stopped 99
get stuck in *traffic* 15
get up 19
get worse 69
give 4
give a bath 6
give back 138
give birth 48
give blood 4
give out 1
go 1
go away 20
go back 125
go bicycling 82
go bowling 82
go dancing 10
go fishing 4
go home 84
go on *a safari* 17
go out 7
go swimming 131
go to sleep 13
grow up 71
grow 2
hammer 79
hand in 23
hand over 15
hang up 6
hang 13
happen 11
have 4
hear 12
help 40
hide 35
hike 22
hire 39

hit 28
hold 44
hold hands 65
hold together 47
hold up 49
hook up 155
hope 49
hurt 50
imagine 50
implant 159
impress 127
improve 71
increase 65
inflate 127
influence 49
inhabit 48
injure 12
insist 157
inspire 49
install 44
interview 49
introduce 47
invade 45
invent 33
invest 81
invite 36
involve 47
irrigate 47
jog 25
keep 93
kid 9
kill 47
kiss 121
knit 89
knock down 38
know 5
last 119
launch 47
lay off 12
leak 7
learn 93
leave 11
leave on 122
liberate 45
lie 127
lie in bed 77
lift weights 72
light up 81
like 5
list 126
listen 79
live 7
locate 48
lock 122
look 8
look forward to 82
lose *my* balance 149
lose 60
love 79
maintain 48
make 6
make a wish 70
make the bed 35
manage 90
march 89
marry 52
mean 53
meet 6
mention 13
miss 20
misunderstand 149
mix up 128
monitor 82

move 5
move away 111
move out 138
mow 92
mug 28
need 6
notice 96
observe 140
offer 37
open 44
operate 159
order 128
oversleep 15
owe 26
own 5
pace 142
paint 33
park 131
participate 12
pass by 70
pay 28
pay attention to 29
pay off 81
perform 12
permit 43
pick out 155
pick up 40
plan 12
plant 13
play 5
play baseball 22
play frisbee 137
point out 28
polish up 125
pour 121
practice 18
prepare 12
preserve 48
press 82
pressure 76
prevent 122
produce 47
program 155
promote 36
protect 159
provide 160
publish 49
pull 47
punch 159
put 28
put up 104
quit 67
rain 13
raise 85
reach 62
read 6
realize 18
rebuild 44
receive 42
record 159
re-elect 97
refuse 15
register 44
regret 67
rehearse 12
reject 37
relate 162
relax 127
remember 26
rent 13
reopen 44
repaint 13
repair 40

185

Irregular Verbs

be	was/were	been	leave	left	left
become	became	become	lend	lent	lent
begin	began	begun	let	let	let
bite	bit	bitten	light	lit	lit
blow	blew	blown	lose	lost	lost
break	broke	broken	make	made	made
bring	brought	brought	mean	meant	meant
build	built	built	meet	met	met
buy	bought	bought	put	put	put
catch	caught	caught	quit	quit	quit
choose	chose	chosen	read	read	read
come	came	come	ride	rode	ridden
cost	cost	cost	ring	rang	rung
cut	cut	cut	run	ran	run
do	did	done	say	said	said
draw	drew	drawn	see	saw	seen
drink	drank	drunk	sell	sold	sold
drive	drove	driven	send	sent	sent
eat	ate	eaten	set	set	set
fall	fell	fallen	sew	sewed	sewed/sewn
feed	fed	fed	shake	shook	shaken
feel	felt	felt	shrink	shrank	shrunk
fight	fought	fought	sing	sang	sung
find	found	found	sit	sat	sat
fit	fit	fit	sleep	slept	slept
fly	flew	flown	speak	spoke	spoken
forget	forgot	forgotten	spend	spent	spent
forgive	forgave	forgiven	stand	stood	stood
freeze	froze	frozen	steal	stole	stolen
get	got	gotten	sting	stung	stung
give	gave	given	sweep	swept	swept
go	went	gone	swim	swam	swum
grow	grew	grown	take	took	taken
hang	hung	hung	teach	taught	taught
have	had	had	tell	told	told
hear	heard	heard	think	thought	thought
hide	hid	hidden	throw	threw	thrown
hit	hit	hit	understand	understood	understood
hold	held	held	wake	woke	woken
hurt	hurt	hurt	wear	wore	worn
keep	kept	kept	win	won	won
know	knew	known	wind	wound	wound
lead	led	led	write	wrote	written

Index